For The
Sake
of My
Sanity

For The Sake

of My

Sanity

YVONNE WHITE

FOR THE SAKE OF MY SANITY

iUniverse books may be ordered through booksellers or by contacting:

iUniverse
1663 Liberty Drive
Bloomington, IN 47403
www.iuniverse.com
844-349-9409

Because of the dynamic nature of the Internet, any web addresses or links contained in this book may have changed since publication and may no longer be valid. The views expressed in this work are solely those of the author and do not necessarily reflect the views of the publisher, and the publisher hereby disclaims any responsibility for them.

Any people depicted in stock imagery provided by Getty Images are models, and such images are being used for illustrative purposes only. Certain stock imagery © Getty Images.

ISBN: 978-1-6632-3456-8 (sc)
ISBN: 978-1-6632-3455-1 (e)

Library of Congress Control Number: 2022918525

Print information available on the last page.

iUniverse rev. date: 05/17/2023

In loving memory of my two kids, Jodi and Mark Clunis.

Contents

Acknowledgments

To my parents, Deloris and Leebert: thank you for the gift of life. To my kids, siblings, and friends who were always there for me. Thanks also to God for the struggles and pain I've faced in my life because if it hadn't been for struggles over the years, I wouldn't be the person I am now.

Thanks to my proofreader, Ms. Shanique Russell, author of *Purpose through Revelation*, who helped me proofread before submitting my book.

Preface

This book was inspired because of my daughter's passing. I never got the chance to grieve because my mind was already fragile from unresolved childhood traumas. Also, it seems like I am drawn to broken men, caused from my own brokenness. My second ex-husband was still living in the same house. Why? When you have been molested as a child, you become overly protective of your children. Even though I didn't want him around me because I'd already lived more than half of my life, I pledged to myself that I would do what I had to do in order to protect my children.

He wasn't allowed to bring his friends, who were addicts, to our home. He couldn't take the children anywhere without letting me know. If I had allowed my own ego to take me over, I wouldn't be able to make the best decisions for the sake of my children.

I plummeted in every area of my life until it felt like things came crushing down on me. I didn't even know that I was dealing with serious depression. My mind was overactive, and it was hard for me to sleep at nights for more than one reason. Many nights, I woke up to the front door ajar, and my ex was nowhere to be found. Stress was my daily bread, and I had this constant fear that something bad was going to happen. I couldn't take stress medication because I always had to be on the alert. I wasn't afraid of him, but I did not trust most of the people he called friends. I will not open that can of worms; that story needs its own trilogy. However, it felt like I was going insane.

I write to maintain my sanity, I had no way of knowing that my son was going to be dead by the time this book would be published. To add insult to injury, COVID-19 showed up just when I thought things couldn't get any worse. COVID-19 sent for its cousin, the Delta variant, with all its baggage, and this was not a hoax.

Poem by My Son, Mark Clunis

A deep breath, even. For this is how to steady a mind. Embrace your peace. Sleep now, my sweet love, for the world will need to be conquered once more. Tomorrow … when your heart is refreshed, mind crisp at the threshold of the returning light of morning … Pick up your sword … The battle awaits.

1

For the Sake of My Sanity

For the sake of my sanity,
I have to find gravity.
I can no longer hide from reality.
I have to find a way to be honest with myself.
It is time to pull myself back up.
For the sake of my sanity, I have to find gravity.

For the sake of my sanity,
I must get back into
The community of the living.
Time for me to stop walking among the living dead.

It is time to stop listening
To the voices in my head,
Like a drum stuck inside my head,
Haunting me and taunting me
While I lay in my bed.

For the sake of my sanity,
I will allow my heavenly Father
To cut off the dry branches in my life

That are stopping me from bearing good fruit.
Lord, please anoint me afresh.

For the sake of my sanity,
Please help me to accept the unacceptable
That is placed on the table of my life.
Please remind me that I had no say in
What was placed on the table of my life
As I came through the passage of birth.
I never chose to be born.
I had no say into who my parents were,
Or what country would be the country of my birth.

It hurts to feel like a leaf blowing in the wind of heartaches and pain.
I'm trying to maintain what is left of myself,
But if I must continue to live,
I have to forgive.

For the sake of my sanity,
Please help me to understand
That forgiving the ones who hurt you
Is not a sign of weakness.
It is for my own peace of mind.

I refuse to continue
To wear unforgiveness around my neck,
Like a slave being dragged about
With chains of bitterness,
Moving from one plantation to the next.

For the sake of my sanity,
I will find the strength to be brave.
I refuse to allow the monster
Called depression to take me to my grave.

Lord, please allow me to wave
The flag of self-forgiveness.
Let me turn my regrets into hopefulness.
For the sake of my sanity, I must walk away from
the wilderness of pain and sorrows.

The winds of calamity will not blow me away.
My life has meaning.
I cannot relive my life.

No starting over,
No clean slate.
the stake is already in the ground.
I am wounded, but I am alive.

No more licking my wounds.
I don't want a new beginning.
All I am asking for is a happy ending
Where I can visit my painful memories
without the pain,
In order to help someone bear their own pain.

Lord, please help me to stop
Looking over my shoulders.
Shower me with your perfect peace.

For the sake of my sanity,

I will find a way to turn my mess into a message.

For the sake of my sanity,

I have to find gravity.

I cannot keep running away from reality.

2

April Fools

Wish that this was a joke,
That COVID-19 was really a hoax.
Then you would not have the need to deal
With people displaying the rush on toilet paper and hand sanitizer.

I wish that this was really a Democratic hoax.
I would not have to be feeling so afraid.
People who died from COVID-19 would still be around,
Maybe flying past you on the freeway.
Chances are they would have given you the middle finger,
And you may tell them where to go and stick it.

No one wants to feel like they are living on borrowed time
And your life is not even worth a dime,
Wondering when it will be your time to die.

Oh, how I wish
That this was really just a joke
And a hoax,
And coronavirus was only a walrus
Wobbling around at the North Pole,

Helping Santa Claus, collecting toys for Christmas,
Floating down the Atlantic Ocean.

Yet here we are wondering
If coronavirus will take
Fifteen months to die down
(No pun intended),
Like the gestation period of a pregnant walrus.

I wish that coronavirus was
A breathing and moving person or thing.
I am sure that the president
Would've already sent a sniper to take it out.
By now we know
He is really good about doing things like that.

Coronavirus is an invisible force
That no one knows how to take out.
Sad to say,
But before anyone can find a cure for this COVID-19,
She will leave a trail of blood
Like this country has never seen
Since World War II.
She's crude.
She is playing by her own sets of rules.
She has no sense of duty.
She will wipe you out
Before you know what hits you.

This is not a joke.
Happy are the ones

Who are already dead.
They don't have to worry about Miss Corona
kissing them on the cheek.
The Bible tells us that the meek
Will inherit the earth.
I wonder how many more bodies Mother Earth will have to bury
By the time COVID-19 gets done.
Only God knows; I don't.
May God help us all.

For now, many are trying
To remember to keep their hands off their noses,
While some are only making
Noises
With the hopes of distracting the voters
Who are lost in a world of unbelief.

Some are still grieving
Over the deaths of their loved ones,
Having to attend virtual funerals.

Many are waiting for the promised check,
Sitting by the mailbox like a fox
Waiting on a prey.
Some folks are still
Exposing themselves and others to COVID-19,
Claiming asking them to wear a mask
Is a violation of their human rights,

Not caring about the next person's
Right to live.

Wish that this was really just a hoax
Brought on by the Dems
Or fake media.
What a confusion.
Am I suffering from delusions?
Is this an April Fools prank?

3

Be Still

B e still for a moment.
Take a little time to unwind.
Don't allow your mind to carry you away to the land of sadness.
Put on the breastplate of righteousness, the helmet of salvation.
Save yourself from the enemy of your soul.

Be still for a moment.
Turn off your cell phone.
Stop postponing
the command of taking control of your thoughts.
Your life is your own.
You are responsible for what you do,
Or what you don't do.

Be still for a moment.
Take an internal shower.
Wash away the dirt of sadness
And regrets.

Fret not thyself
About those who continue to do evil
In the name of getting rich.

Remember that riches sometimes take flight and soar into heaven
On the wings of fire,
Leaving you holding on to the smoke.

Be still for a moment.
Take a little time to rewind
And connect with your soul again.

4

Pain

Pain is a painful reminder
of what life is all about.
It is not fair to lose a child.
No parent ever wants to bury a child,
But sometimes it happens,
and it rips your heart to pieces.

Sometimes it literally
feels like someone have a knife inside your stomach,
twisting and turning it inside of you
while you lay in your bed at nights,
trying to fall asleep,
trying to close out the memories,

hoping and praying
that your eyes
will help you to escape.
You close your eyes, trying to fall asleep.
Why do you still see
your child's face looking at you in the distance?
You reach out
to touch your child, yet you can't.

You need extra-long arms,
so you grab a stick with a hook
to pull your child in.
You drop the stick and you scream,
"No! No!"

You try to swim across to reach your child,
only to wake up
pulling on your hair that's already falling out
from stress and the pain of losing a child.
Your heart is beating—beating too fast,
really, really fast.
You're tired,

tired as if you never sleep.
Your sheet is lying on the floor,
and you are screaming out to God, "Please
take this pain away from me!"

5

How Much Can I Bear?

Sometimes you literally feel
like you just want to die.
Because the pain is too much to bear.
My dear,
Who said that you have to bear it all on your own?
Reach out talk to someone,
Anyone.
It is time for you to talk to someone
About how you are feeling.
It is okay for you to not be okay.
Talking to someone
About how you are feeling
Is not seeking pity.

God created us to lean on each other.
Yes, everyone
Has their own bag of pain
They are carrying. Sharing is caring.
Looking for someone
To share your sorrows with
Is different from looking for pity.

Please open the window to your heart
And the windows in your house.

Let's start the healing by cleaning.
Your child is never coming back,
Not in this lifetime,
So it is time to heal
And clean up
Your heart
And your house.

Open your curtains,
Open your heart.
Let the sun
Come into your house
and the Son
Come into your heart.

Feel the sunshine,
Experience the peace of God.
Allow Him to put your broken heart back together again
From the pain of loss.

6

Emotional Closets

It is twelve days to Christmas,
And I am trying really hard to mask the sadness
That comes around this time of year.
What do I mean by masking?
Well, you have to find a way to escape from the place of sadness
That sits inside your heart.

Been through a lot of sadness
Over the course of becoming a woman.
I now have the courage
To open up my emotional closets
And get rid of things that have been weighing me down.

This is the second Christmas
Since my daughter passed away.
Last year,
I was like a dead woman walking.
I was not even sure that I would live to see this year.

That being said,
As a mother, I truly love my children.
So in the middle of walking beneath an avalanche of hot, bitter tears

And leaning up against the wall of sadness,
Something inside me reminded me that dying would help me.
I would not feel sad anymore.
But what about my children?
What would happen to them?

I think I truly understand
Why I have my two youngest children.
God is using them
To pull me out of depression.

I know it's almost Christmas.
I know I will be all right eventually.

I have to stay alive for my other children and grandchildren.
Depression is real, but I will beat it.
I know that I am never going to be the same again.
It's twelve days until Christmas. Why does it feel
like I am twelve feet under the ground?

7

Christmas Eve

It is Christmas Eve, and I am feeling weak.
I don't always feel this way,
Or maybe I just don't try to stay in the zone of sadness.

This is the second Christmas since my
daughter bade this world goodbye.
And I became a walking dead,
Feeling like an outcast,
Like bacon in a skillet.
I am getting fried,
And the tears from my eyes
Drip from my tear ducts,
Making sizzling sounds
That no one can hear.
Even as my hair breaks off in the comb,
I pine away with unhappy memories
And worries of years gone by

Feeling alone doesn't mean that no one loves or cares for you.
It is just the way you feel.
Why don't you meet me
Right where I'm at,

In the bed of sorrows,
In the depths of despair
In the corn field of regrets
called
"The fields of opportunity"?

As I wander the streets of loneliness
Trying to cling to happiness,
I am crippled by sadness

Buried deep inside of me
From yesteryears,
Following me around like a chained-up, wounded dog
Whose tail has been tied
Between his legs to his collar,
Without a voice to bark.

Why don't you meet me where I'm at?
Sit with me.
Let's talk.

No, this is not your turn to talk.
I need you to listen.
I get it—it's hard to listen to a person like me
who has a million things to unload.

You don't have the time to listen,
But more importantly,
You don't have the room for my extra junk.
Your trunk is
Already full of your own junk.

Why do you even ask me how I'm feeling
When you know
That you don't have the time to listen
To what I have to say?

Why don't you meet with me
Right where I'm at?

It's Christmas Eve,
And I am shaking like a leaf,
Feeling so weak.

8

Christmas Day

Not sure if I should say
It's been my worst Christmas.
I went to work,
did what I had to do.
They don't even
have a clue as to what I am going through.
I feel so empty.
It's almost like something
has gutted me out.
Like an old house that has been
demolished from the inside out.

They say that time
will heal your wounds.
What I would like to know
is how long will it take for me
to heal from the pain
In the bottom of my heart
that refuses to go away.

The loneliness,
the sadness,

the longing that I am experiencing.
I know that I am not the only one
who is feeling a sense of grief.
The problem is
I don't fully understand the process of grief.

Tell me how I stop
my bleeding heart from beating so fast.
Sometimes it is hard to breathe,
hard to talk about how I'm feeling.
Sometimes it seems
like I can't even feel.
I am trying to stop these feelings
of wanting to stop feeling.
Tell me how long
before I succumb to the weight of the burden
of this thing called grief.
Will my parents have to bury me too?

I know that I am strong,
that God still loves me,
and eventually
I'm going to be OK.
But until then,

I just want to run away
and hide myself from these feelings of excruciating pain,
like someone is pounding
nails inside my heart.

It is Christmas Day,
And I am screaming,
"Mayday! Mayday!"
But no one can help me.
No one can take away
the pain I am feeling or stop
my heart from bleeding.
The good book says
that weeping may endure for a night,
but joy cometh in the morning.

For now, I am in mourning,
waiting for the morning,
when the light called happiness will take me to happier times.

I guess time will tell
if all will be well.
Right now, I am drowning
in a well of sadness,
watching my hair fall off
my head like autumn leaves,
with my neck pulled into my shell
like a turtle.
Slowly crawling, slowly dying,
trying to reach the other side
of the mountain,
where life holds new meaning.
But until then, my heart keeps bleeding.
Yes! I am sure:
this is the worst Christmas of my life.

I feel like I just want
to curl up and bawl in a corner.

I find myself asking God,
How much more I can take?

I am sitting at the door of insanity.
Not sure if you are listening to me.
If you are,
please help me to deal with this thing called grief!
It is Christmas Day
Please grant me this wish.

9
You

Everything is always about you.
You are the universe;
The universe is in you.
You are the cake.
You are the egg in the cake.
You take and you bake, you shake and you take.

You are the eyeball in the middle of the face.
You spread fear.
You see only yourself.
You are a self-made god.
You use power to force people to serve you.

One day you're going to realize that
You are not the universe.
You cause a lot of adversity,
But when Judgment Day comes,
And believe me, it's coming,
You will realize that you are not the universe.
You are just another man,
Another man who sees himself as God.
Remember Jim Jones.

How can it be that all you see
Is what you see?
People are dying.
Many are crying.
Tear gas is flying.
But all you can ask me is how I think you are doing,
While people are fearing for their lives.

Did anyone ever tell you
That the way to get people to serve you is to serve them?
You cannot force people to serve you.
They will only serve you because you make them,
But they will not be serving you from the heart.
Stop blowing the dog whistle.
When and how will this madness end?
How many will have to lie dead before you get it in your head
That you are just another man?
You are not God.

When will the killing cease?
How many will have to die
Before you see that words have consequences?
How can it be that you are serving the people
While at the same time, you are serving their
heads on your platter of hate?
They cannot stand at your gate,
Because if they do, you give orders to shoot them.
You treat them like leaves blowing in the wind.

Wheeling and dealing,
Kneeling on the neck of justice

While you have your ego for breakfast, lunch, and dinner.
Your minions without opinions are enabling you,
Putting the label of soon-to-be king on your chest.

The country is trying to digest the mess
That is coming out of your mouth.
Watching you motioning to the Klansmen,
Putting them on standby,
Generating anger and fear.

Who are you?
When and how will this madness end?
How many will have to lie dead before you get it in your head
That you are just another man?
You are not God.
Are you even a human being?
Why does everything always have to be about you?

10

Fatally Speaking

Fatally speaking,
from the grave, can anyone explain the meaning of the madness
behind the system of justice?
Some of those who called themselves peace officers
are nothing but cowards,
wearing blue without a clue as what to do,
to maintain law and order.

Stop them from creating disorder.
The trigger-happy police would have to take a back
seat behind Barney Fife in Mayberry.
What happened to the level-headed Andy Griffiths
when it comes to stopping mayhem
from ripping the hem from law and order?

Fatally speaking,
from the grave,
if you are a coward,
you should never become a peace officer.
You make all the good police
look like villains.

My neighbor called you
because he was worried about my safety.
My door was ajar.
He, being a good neighbor,
sounded the alarm by calling the peace officers,
who had nothing to offer
but bullets from their guns.

Then you wonder why black folks run
when they see you coming.
The danger we feel is real.
Law and order have been stealing
our lives for a very long time.

What was my crime?
Or better yet,
what was my name?
To many of you, this is just a game.
I say it is a shame
that taxpayers have to pay people like you
to dig holes in the justice system
In the name of God knows what.

Fatally speaking,
from the grave,
what did you write in your report
about your encounter with me
on that fateful night?
The world may forget,
but my family will not.

Because of you,
I am placed in the ground to rot.
My blood will never be enough to satisfy
the bloodthirsty demons
who roam around seeking innocent blood.

You came to my neighborhood.
I was not wearing a hoodie.
I was not a hood rat.
I was not in your space sucking up your air.
Do you think it is fair for you to end my life
before I have a chance to live?

I know that my family will forgive you,
Because in God we believe,
And He tells us in His words
that we have to forgive.
Forgive me for asking,
but I really want to know.
How much more innocent blood
have you already shed?

My blood has a voice.
You took my life.
My voice is silent,
but my blood is speaking.
Cain could not hide from the face of God,
Even if your lawyers manage to convince the jury
that you had a valid reason to kill me inside
my house with my nephew watching.

God is watching you.
You will one day have to answer to Him.

Fatally speaking,
from the grave,
my life matters.

11

He Don't Care

So you really think that he cares?
If you think he does, then you are dumber than a bunch
of rocks riding on the back of uneducated fool.

He don't care.
Stop wasting your time
trying to pour water into a broken vessel.
Stop trying to fill his cup with stupidity.
If you don't, you will be flooded with water
from the dam of condemnation.

He don't care.
He loves the confrontation.
Creating confusion and mayhem is his game
Don't you see he is hard to tame?
He is all about playing the blame game;
that is how he gains fame.
He is in the business of fanning the flame
of hate,
spreading division.

This is not an illusion.
Get used to the new norm.
Sorry to break it to you:
They don't care.
Do you?

12

In Trouble Again

In trouble again.
What did you do?
Nothing.

Sitting on the sideline of life
with no hopes and dreams
will get you in more trouble than if you were taking active part
in this thing we call life.

In a hurry, looking for curry.
Currying favor will get you into more trouble than you bargained for.
In trouble again.

13

Stop

Stop holding on to the past.
Find the bridge to your happiness.
Stop wallowing in self-pity,
Yes, life has been unkind to you.
The big question is, Have you been kind to yourself?

Stop trying to control the uncontrollable.
You will find yourself slipping on dry ground when
you should be standing on dry ground.

Stop allowing people
To treat you like your life don't matter.
Why should people treat you with respect when you
have not yet learned how to respect yourself?

Stop holding on to the past.
Live in the moment.
Why do you convince yourself
That you are the only one having heartaches and pain?
Stop wearing your pain on your sleeve.
Leave the mess behind you.

If you can't leave it behind you,
let your mess become your message.

Stop massaging your fear.
Dry your tears.
Face life with understanding.
Stop expecting people to like you
while secretly you still hate yourself.

You are an agent of change.
All you need to know
to succeed in life is to accept yourself,
flaws and all.
Find a way to get beyond your fears.
Stop holding on to your fears.

14

Who Are You?

Who are you to judge me?
To tell me who to be
and not to be?
Why are you so busy
interfering in my affairs?

My life is not a fairytale.
I have much to fear.
I choose to walk past my fears.
I'm not looking back.
Whatever you have to say to me,
have the balls to look me
in the eyes and tell me what you have to say to my face.

Who are you to keep belittling me,
making me out to be a monster
without feelings
when you have no way
of really understanding what makes me tick?
You are like a tick
on my back,
slowly draining my blood.

Are you not tired
of swimming in my blood?
Who are you to judge me,
to tell me
who to be?

15

In a Hurry

In a hurry,
trying to scurry.
Wish I had some chicken to curry,
Instead of eating brisket.
Life's a treat,
they say.

You should treat it with respect.
In trouble again.
What did you do? Nothing.

Sitting on the sidelines
of life with no hope or dreams will get you in more trouble
than if you were taking an active part in the thing they call life.
In a hurry, trying to scurry.

16

So You Think

So you think that you
have the answers
to the question of all questions
of how to be happy?
How to lose weight,
and even how to get to heaven?

Do you have the answer
to how to act when you are eleven,
and adults want to treat you like you are twenty-one?

I'm only eleven.
I am going through changes.
My voice is changing.
I am changing.
So you still think you have to try to change me
Why do I need to fit in?
Not expecting you to have an answer to all my questions.
I just want to be able to ask questions
without being judged or told to shut up.

So you still think you know me?
Right now, friendship means more to me than learning.
I know that I will get into trouble for being strong-willed,
for talking back.
Don't even know why you call it talking back.

So you think that I am
nothing but a troublemaker.
Not because I don't listen right away.
Doesn't means I am not hearing and learning.
I have a lot on my mind.
What bothers me the most
is you are expecting me to learn
the lessons you are teaching me,
yet you get offended if I question you.

I am truly sorry if I make you mad
by asking you why I should do,
or not to do.
What you are telling me to do?

I am growing up too fast.
My brain is trying to catch up with my body.
I have many questions;
I only need one answer at a time.
Please give me space
and time to get to the place
where I can understand
the meaning of life.

For now, all I am trying to do
is get to know who I am.

Sorry, I don't have the answers
to why I don't always listen.
May I remind you
that I am only eleven years old?

17

Hear Me

Hear me out.
Sit with me.
Let me tell you
what this is all about.

I am at the roundabout in a busy town
listening to the honking of horns,
watching people acting like animals in a barn.
Dashing to the store to
buy a piece of happiness
while leaving crumbs of sadness
that lead to their front door.

Will you please hear me out?
You can't buy happiness;
it is not for sale on Amazon/
It is only the amazing
grace of Jesus that can give you happiness.
Sad to say that the road to happiness sometimes takes us

through the back door of sadness.
Hear me out.

If you give God a chance, he will show you
how to turn your mess into a message.

18

Why?

Why, why, why?
Everyone likes to ask why'
even though we don't always
want to know why.
It is hard to understand that
life sometimes doesn't give us
the reason why.

All my life, I have been asking why.
Why?
Why?
Why?
Now, I think I know why
my eyes will not let me see,
my ears will not let me hear,
my mind will not let me forget,
even though I wish it would.
I still find myself
wanting to know why.

We live in a world of confusion,
where many are suffering from delusion,

trying to come to their own conclusions
of not wanting to know why,
even though they
find themselves asking why.
If we were able to know why,
you would tell me that life holds no guarantee;
here today, gone tomorrow,
sometimes before we take the time to live.

"Why?"
is the question
we shouldn't even ask,
because we don't want to know why.
Asking why
Is not just for five-year-olds.
It is for all of God's children.
Sometimes asking him, Why?
Why?
Why?
Does everyone want to know why?

19

How?

God, how can I stand on your promises?
How can I prove to myself
that you love me?
Help me to remember
that I am not alone.

How do I cope,
cope
with all the brokenness?
How can I cope
with this dark cloud that is hovering over me?
You have to face them head-on/
Just because you find

a way to get around your heart aches and pain
doesn't mean that you don't have to deal with them.
Unresolved issues
will allow you to fall over the edge of life,
slowly eating you out from the inside.
Only you and God know your heart.
Only you and God can solve the troubles of your soul.

20

The Race

In loving memory of my sister, Angella Graham-Stewart

How to finish the race and save face?
Find a way to embrace the author and finisher of your faith.
Follow after peace;
it will take you through
the valley of understanding.
While you are at the valley of understanding,
try to fill your cup with patience.
When you do,
you will start to bear the fruit of love and respect.

How to finish the race and save face?
learn to be grateful and graceful,
even when you are being battered
by the storm of rejection.
Forget the *-isms* and schisms.
Bring your own lunch to the table of life.
Share your faith with the ones who need it.
Find a way to walk in love and unity
if you want to unify
the spirit of brotherhood

and sisterhood
in the community
of love and unity.

Everyone seems to be
looking out for number one, racing toward anarchy
without stopping to think
about the monarch butterflies
Spreading their tiny wings,
migrating to Texas before the brutal
winter from the Midwest
cast its spell upon the little brown church,
covering the steeple with snowflakes.

If God cares about tiny butterflies,
why are you even doubting his love for you?
Please, try to remember
that God will take care of you.
Find your vest of compassion,
wear it to protect your heart from becoming callous.
Let love live in the neighborhood.
Let's finish the race with grace
with love by our side.
That's how you finish the race and save face.

21

Cope

Dedicated to My Angel

How do I cope when all I am feeling is hopelessness?
Where can I go when it feels like my life is over,
And every day is just another sad existence?

People insist on telling you
that everything is going to be OK
without taking the time to understand what you are going through.

Do you even understand what it feels like to lose your firstborn?
That was the face you look on to know that you are a mother,
A pink bundle of joy.
Your little girl, looking up at you
as she latches onto your breast.
Because of her, I put the past behind me,
or at least I thought I did.

Seems like my painful childhood memories were dug up again.
While they were putting her in the grave,
I was trying to be brave.

Now, I know that I should have screamed and rolled in the dirt.
Why did I not hold my belly and bawl?

Now, I find myself crawling;
the little girl in me is calling
upon the woman I am becoming
never to forget the wounded little girl
who is still waiting for emancipation.

The only way to free her
is to give her a voice.
Please, I am begging you: stop running away from the girl in you.
If you were given a chance
to heal from being molested,
you wouldn't be feeling like someone tied a
heavy stone around your neck,
dropping you at the bottom of Lake Hopelessness.
Now, you are carrying the pain of the woman and the
suffering of the wounded girl hiding in side of you.

Now that I am living in a cornfield
far, far
away from family that loves me,
some are even wondering
if I have forgotten to good old days,
when I was the one whom many would come to for help and advice.
How and when will I be able
to explain to them,
that I don't know who I am anymore?

The Yvonne you knew
is no longer around;,
like a glass bowl
that has been placed into the oven of sorrows, the oven was too hot.
I am shattered in a million tiny pieces.
Yvonne, your daughter;
Yvonne, your mother;
Yvonne, your sister and friend—
she is never ever coming back,
unless God gives her a comeback.

Jodi was my pride and joy
from day one.
I knew that I would do all I could
to make her life better than mine was;
it was not about me anymore.

With no mother to tell me
what to do
or not to do,
you learn to do what you have to do
to care for the love of your life.
Jodi, you were so beautiful,
not to mention smart.

Sometimes I wish
that I could have traded places with you,
but that's not how it works.
Only God alone can tell
why things don't go the way we plan them,
and why we have to go through such hell.

Jodi,

I know that you are not feeling any pain because you are dead,

yet I cannot get you out of my head.

This is new for me.

I have no idea

how long the pain is going to last.

How do you cope when you are feeling hopeless?

I will try to have peace because that's

what you would want me to have, as well as hope.

I will do my best, my angel.

22

I Can't Breathe

Inspired by Social Issues

The mother in me is outraged.
I can't breathe.
I have the need to engage with the murderers who wear blue.
Not saying that all blue shirters are murderers.
I can't breathe.
I have a voice through the tip of my pen,
and I can't cage these emotions anymore.

I can't breathe.
Why would you kneel on his neck
like you were kneeling at the throne of hostility,
and you were doing exorcism to cleanse the earth
from the evil called George Floyd?
A black man saying,
I can't breathe!
I can't breathe!
Your face, Mr. Blue Shirt, tells another story.
It said that you would not be able to breathe
Until you stop him from breathing.
I can't breathe.

For more than nine minutes, you pressed on his neck.

What the heck?

Just because he used a counterfeit twenty-dollar bill.

I can't breathe.

Did you even stop to think that maybe someone else gave it to him?

Was that a crime?

If your answer is yes,

did he deserve the death penalty?

I can't breathe!

People get jail time for leaving their dogs into a hot car,

get labeled animal abusers.

Many find it amusing to watch police killing a person of color.

I can't breathe!

A dog wearing a collar has more rights than a black man!

If Michael Vick had to do jail time for dog fights,

what makes you think you have the right to take George Floyd's life?

In the name of what?

Fearing for your life?

I can't breathe!

Have you ever heard about innocent until proven guilty?

How could I forget—being black makes you

guilty even after proven innocent.

I can't breathe!

Mr. Blue Shirts,

I know that you are not all murderers,

but if you look the other way while your colleague commits murder,

what does that make you?

I can't breathe!

No one raises a finger, not even a pinky,
in defense of a black man whose life has been cut short.
Could it be that you guys are running a cult?

I can't breathe!
I can't breathe!
How many times have you killed a man
in the name of power and brutality,
Mr. Blue Shirt?
Do you have children?
If you do, can you honestly look them in the
eyes without feeling a sense of guilt?
Or will you use the splatter of the black man's blood
to make yourself a quilt of hostility
to shield yourself from the outcry of the black community?

I can't breathe!
I can't breathe!
Seems to be the hallmark and an anthem
that black men have to sing
as their bodies sink
in the abyss of utter darkness with the hand
of injustice upon their necks.
I can't breathe!
Not to mention those who get shot in the back
because blue shirts were scared
of getting killed by black men fleeing for their lives.
I can't breathe!

I guess black lives don't matter,
so you will just keep serving their heads on a platter,

because too many see black folks as just squatters,
so they call out the SWAT,
yelling, Step back,
let the chief of craftiness through
with his sword in hand.
To him, they say, power belongs,
reminding us that white
is always right.
You are the knight with power and might
I can't breathe!

I stand corrected,
but I have a gut feeling
that while you were kneeling
on his neck, you were sending a message
to Colin Kaepernick.
Many take offense to him taking a knee
to protest the treatment of black men by police.
You have a look of defiance on your face,
not even a trace or concern in your eyes.
Is it because George had a white girlfriend
That you take offense to his existence?

I can't breathe!
Your eyes were cold,
like you belonged in *The Walking Dead*.
You are heartless.
Because of you, many are having
an out-of-body experience,
trying to wake up from the nightmare

of watching someone being tortured on national TV.
I can't breathe!

The mother in me is outraged.
I can no longer cage these emotions.
I can't breathe!
I can't breathe!
Who is going to be the next victim?
I can't breathe!
I can't breathe!
Who will stand up and speak out against
police brutality?

It is not from a lack of standing up.
When black lives matters take to the street
to protest the killing of another black man,
they are met with tear gas.
You pump them with rubber bullets.
You create more hostility in the black community.

I can't breathe!
I can't breathe!
To you, this is a game.
You are trying to appeal to your base,
using the heads of black men and boys
like they are balls for you to kick around!
I can't breathe!
I can't breathe!
Mammy!
Mammy!
I can't breathe!

But the last words he heard,
as you apply more pressure to his windpipe,
is, "If you can talk, you can breathe."

The mother in me is outraged.
I need to engage.
George Floyd was not a pig.
Still, he has been fried in the skillet
like bacon
while you labeled him as being a troublemaker and a drug addict.
Makes me wonder
if some of you are working
for the undertaker.
I can't breathe!
I can't breathe!
I hope you know that one day,
you too will have to answer to your maker.

I can't breathe!
I can't breathe!
So go ahead,
create more mayhem,
call out the paper tigers.
That is what you are good at.
Make up another report;
you are a hero,
and black men are zero.
Just so you know,
zero is the greatest number
in the world.
George Floyd is gone.

His voice will never be silenced
I can't breathe!
I can't breathe!
Let's take a slice from life.
Please find a way to end the strife.

Brace yourself;
the world will never be the same again.
Funny how some people
are of the opinion that if he had
not spoken to the police,
he would not have been dead.
When are you going to get it in your head?
Martin Luther King was peaceful.
That did not save him from the bullet that ended his life.

What did Marcus Garvey do
to deserve being labeled a criminal?

We are at a new terminal.
The younger generation
have fire in their blood.
They are boiling.

Social media is their meeting ground.
They are smarter than you.
Stop thinking about what to do.
Just do what you know is right.
And if you don't have a clue as to what you have to do,
stop trying to spray crazy glue inside the heads of the headless,

programming them to see
only what you want them to see.

A sea of emotions
is about to sweep the country.
It will spread across the world.
Nothing will be able to stop
the people from showing their emotions;
not even COVID-19
will be able to stop what is about to happen.

How do I know?
I feel it in my bones,
like a person who has arthritis knows when it is getting cold
before the TV person reads the weather.

I think that God himself
is saying,
I can't breathe!
What happened to the people
I have created?

The mother in me is outraged.
I have the need to engage.
This is my constructive way
to deal with these raging emotions.
It is hard for me to breathe,
watching George Floyd
take his last breath on the pavement,
in payment
for not complying to the demands of a peace officer

who was on the defense,
leaning on the fence
of compulsiveness
while taking away the rights
of another human being,
putting out his light,
claiming that you are right
because being white in a blue shirt gives you the right
to rob him of his life.

It is even harder to listen to people talking
from both corners of their mouths,
belching out fire and fury against anyone.

Who dares to speak out against police brutality
in defense of a black man or woman?

My black family,
My white friends,
please, stop and breathe.
Yes, take a deep breath.
Please, I am begging you.
Don't burn any buildings,
don't go stealing from the stores.

I know that the Bible tells us that the devil
comes to steal and to destroy.
So don't allow them to label us as looters,
don't give them a reason to shoot.

Even though you and I both know
that they are programmed to kill
in the name of power and might.

Seems like some of them
can't breathe
if they don't stop someone from breathing.

My heart is bleeding.
All lives matter.
Black lives matter.
Please, stop the splattering of our blood.

George Floyd told you that he couldn't
breathe,
but you kept your foot on his neck
just because you see yourself
as an earthly god.
It will not be long before you will have to answer to the law.

I want to remind you
That God is the ultimate judge and the official jury.
In time you will reap your reward.

George's mother is not alive
to mourn his death,
but all the mothers of the world
will mourn for him.

We, the black mothers
living in the United States of America,

will not be able to breathe
until we know that our children
will not be slaughtered in the streets
or shot while lying on their sheets in their beds.

We cannot get the image out of our heads.
Will my child be the next victim?

The mother in me is outraged.
I cannot cage these emotions anymore.
I can't breathe!
I can't breathe!

23

It's Time to Talk

Dear God, It's time for me to be free.
I have been carrying this load
for way too long.

Now, I feel like the wind of time is carrying me away
to places I don't want to go.
The question is how
must I get away from all the drama and traumas?

It is what it is,
and this is what it is.
I am tired of all the inward fighting
and lying to myself about how I am feeling
and not feeling.
Feels like I am locked into a mental cage,
Trying to disengage my brain,
trying to forget the past.
But everywhere I go, it seems
like it keeps following me trying to strangle me.

I really want to move on.
It seems like the door to my past is jammed,

and no matter what I do, I cannot shut it.
Where does that leaves me?

I am trapped in a world of sad emotions,
motioning for help, yet no one
seems to take the bait.
If only they knew what I am going through,
wondering what will be my fate.

The problem is
they are reaching out to me,
but I now reside on an island
where alligators are swimming around me
with hungry, angry eyes,
like John on the island of Patmos.
God is telling me to write my story
because he is going to use me to reach someone,
somewhere out there, who is thinking that no one cares
about what they are going through.
Maybe you are about to
squeeze the trigger to take your life.
Stop! You don't have to do that.
Talk to someone about how you are feeling.

Happiness is a happy word
spoken sometimes by people
who have no clue to what happiness really means.
Many write songs about it,
trying to grasp the meaning of happiness
while they live in a world of sadness,
doing all they can to act happy

with the hope the world won't find about the dark side
that they tried so hard to hide.

How do you know if a person is truly happy?
Is it in the song they write or sing,
the way they smile?
Or is it because they go the extra mile to be kind?

If someone else apart from my kids is reading this,
that means I did find the courage to publish my
second collection of poems or thoughts.
I don't think that I am the only one who has problems;
compared to some, my troubles are small.

For me, at times I feel like I want to crawl
under a rock and never come out!
If there was a rock that could hide a person from the troubles of life,
I am sure that it is already taken.

Jesus is the only rock that I have to lean on.
I often feel like He too has abandoned me.
I sometimes blame Him for sitting back
and allowing me to feel so much pain!

But somehow I know that I have to learn how to trust Him
with what's felt of my life.
There is no way around what I am going
through and about to go through.
I just have to trust and hope that He knows what He is doing.

I know that He knows everything.
I am the one who will have to let go
of the baggage that I carry around,
or should I say that is now dragging me around.

How will I let go of the pain and hurt that keeps me up at nights?
Who is right and who is wrong? At whose feet will I lay the blame?
Whom will I share the pain and hurt with.

Where must I go to find myself, or what is left of me?
Should I just roll over and play dead?
Or must I start acting like I am just an ordinary
fool who is just trying to play it cool?

The children of my youth are no longer young.
They are growing up while I am growing down, trying to
hold the peace at the expense of my own happiness.

Sometimes I feel
like I am just a bird
who has lost its nest with all the eggs.
I am flying around trying to see where my eggs will hatch.
No one even notice what I am going through
Just because I refused to complain about myself.
Sometimes my heart is so heavy that I have to stop and rest
while resisting the temptation to throw in the towel.

Do you ever get the feeling that you are sitting on the edge of insanity?
Trying to hold on to reality,
only to have gravity trip you up,
and you find out that life is mostly unfair,

and not everyone who asks you how you
are doing really wants to know?

Knowing what I know now,
I do not ask how come I feel the way I do.
Now I know why.
If you grew up
not having anyone to talk to about your feelings,
you learn not to trust anyone with your deep emotions.
You tend to fly off in a corner by yourself,
trying to deal with your emotions
without creating a commotion.

But in doing so,
you are robbing yourself
of the bond of friendship from family
and from people who love you.

So if it is possible, please do yourself a favor.
Find someone to talk to about
whatever you went through and are still going through.
You cannot wish it away.
Being raped or molested just don't go away.
You may put it in a corner somewhere inside your mind,
but it's there knocking, whispering, reminding
you that it is still unresolved.
It is time to talk.

24

Mistrust

Distraction will come at a time when you are not expecting it,
causing ripples in the water of unexpected heartaches,
leaving you to pick up the pieces of sadness and loneliness,
watching self-righteous people
treat you like you're the scum of the earth
while they try to uproot you from the only life you know.

But the harder they try,
the harder you should try to keep your identity.
Remember that you are a member of the community of the living.
You have a right to exist in a world that was
created by God for all to enjoy.

Don't be in a hurry to start a war that will not finish in your lifetime,
committing crimes and not expecting to be charged for it,
deploying your spies to kill,
teaching them to lie,
hiding behind the veil of you are right and everyone else is wrong.

It won't be long before you realize that
everyone has their version of the truth.
Sometimes you must learn to take a back seat

to really focus on what is going on.

Look, listen, and learn.

If you do, you will learn to speak with understanding.

Then you will be able to stand up to the naysayers in your life.

Who likes to tell you that you will never become anything?

Distraction will come, but remember to stay focused on the prize.

In Loving Memory of My Nephew Kenrick,
Affectionately Known as Kurtis

K—Kind

U—Understanding

R—Respectful

T—Trustworthy

I—Intelligent

S—"Scotch bonnet pepper mixed with dark chocolate

25

Knowing

Knowing when to walk away,
knowing when to fight
or to take flight,
might save your life.
Knowing when to shut up,
knowing when to speak,
may help you win the war over the enemy of your soul.

Learning how to be humble is a gift from God.
To stay humble, you have to resist the urge to grumble and complain.
Contentment is a gift from God;
anyone can receive it just by asking.

Instruction belongs to the wise;
foolishness is a bedrock for fools.
Who uses their tongues like a hoe,
To dig for themselves holes?
It will not be long before they fall into it.
Knowing who you are is the first step to
becoming who God created you to be.

Dreams without tears are easy to achieve.
Some dreams take blood sweat and tears
to climb the staircase to greatness.

Knowing when to say you are sorry
sometimes is all you need to know.
Knowing who you are is one of the main ingredients
that you need to succeed in life.
Don't you ever give up on your dreams.

The system is trying to break you
by squeezing you,
demanding more from you.
Don't sacrifice your self-worth
like a Woolworth's department store
peddling its many mismatches, trying to catch your attention.

Seducing you, trying to reduce you to the rubble of worthlessness,
acting like your life is a contest they won and you have lost,
like you don't have the right to be treated like a human being.

Knowing who you are is always going to be the main ingredients
you will need to get where you need to be.
Knowing when to walk away is sometimes all you need to know.

26

Lawlessness

Inspired by Social Issues

Lawlessness law with too many flaws,

flowing in the streets.
Lawless law beating its drum:
Boodum boodum!
Boodum dum dum!

Lawless law
living in the attic of a crowded mind,
hiding from the truth, acting like a common fool.
Opening up the floodgates to folks who
have no sense of wrong or right,
banging the drums of contempt.
Meanwhile, contemplating ripping up the
constitution in the name of hocus-pocus,
trying to shift the focus from the elephant in in room.

Lawless law that has no claws, clueless to fairness,
creating a brawl, trying to paint the room with water gating,

navigating the muddy streams of lies and deceptions
while inviting the uninvitables to come and eat vegetables.

Filling up the swamp
with a bunch of minions without opinions,
with mouths that move only in the direction
of defending the chief of craftiness.
Pretending that they are blind dogs—
see no evil, speak no evil, do evil.
Barking from morning to evening,
trying to get even with naysayers.

Lawlessness is blooming while they continue to build a house of lies,
trying to bribe and hide behind the walls of immunity.
Fixing to start a riot in the community,
hiding from reality.
Presiding over communities of hackers and haters,
acting like mules yet expecting everyone to play it cool.

Lawlessness, lawlessness,
beating their drums:
boodum boodum, boodum boodum dum dum!
While more people are climbing the peach tree, shaking it, shaking it,
Waiting to hear "Timber"
to watch the dust rise to the clouds.
While some are waiting in the streets
to sweep the memory of lawful days in the culvert of king after all.

Lawlessness will not rest
until everyone knows that he is the chief of his unbridled imagination
who refused to attend orientation,

giving out citation
in the name of hell and powerhouse.
Lawlessness is a spirit
That is marching across the land,
beating his drum:
boodum boodum dum!

27

Sitting

Sitting in the lobby, practicing
patience,
trying to pretend that I know what I am doing.
Standing at the roundabout of heartaches and pain,
trying to explain
my pain away.
Sitting in the lobby of yesteryears,
wondering why the world is tilting upside down.
Why are some folks living on downer,
Like toner in a printer, squinting and squinting,
trying to keep the tears behind their eyelids?

Sitting in the lobby of not knowing what to do,
thinking about our to-do list that never gets done,
feeling like a black cat.
Sitting in the Georgia dome on Halloween night,
trying to shake off the gloom and doom
waiting for the flowers to bloom.

Sitting in the lobby of
wanting to be more than just a wannabe
searching for peace

while waging war against my heart,
even as my brain try to dissect the images that flows through my head,
lying in my bed,
trying to will my mind to stay still and get well.

Sitting under the backdrop of insanity,
trying to reason with logic.
I end up getting colic from
eating too much
yet starving for more.
Morally speaking I am far from perfect.
Yet I'm striving to perfection
only to uncover my imperfections,
fighting with perplexity
of the complexity,
of dealing with my anxieties.

Trying to fight this thing they call coronavirus,
Like Paul and Silas,
who prayed their way out of prison.
I will shout it from the mountaintop:
my mind's made up; I am never going to give up.
I will keep looking up to my heavenly father,
seeking his wisdom to show me what to do.

Sitting in the lobby of lamentation,
trying to face the reality
that my life as I knew it
will never be the same again.
I am wasting away,
feeling like a castaway.

My full-time job is to glorify God in the beauty of his holiness.
Yet I am lost in the wilderness
of not knowing what to do or where to turn.

God is working on our behalf.
He will show us what to do and when to do it.
I'm sitting in the lobby of my identity,
ready to face reality.
Pain and sorrows are also a part of my everyday reality.

Sitting in the lobby
of pain and suffering,
not wanting to talk to anyone,
while speaking to everyone,
hoping to find a magic wand to wave away my sorrows.
I am being weighed on the scale called life,
tilting too much to one side,
Sliding into depression,
hiding at the brook
of my daughter's grave,
not wanting to talk to anyone.

Living in a white world
filled with strangers.
Feeling like a grain of black pepper
in the salt shaker.
Like a fly in a jug of milk,
milking my fears,
drinking my tears,
losing my hair,
sitting in the lobby,
waiting, lounging, but I know I will overcome.

28

Love Is a Song

Love will never bow down
and serve evil or hide behind
the veil of loving some and hating some.
Love and hate cannot dwell in the same house.

You are either a lover or a hater;
love will remain the same.
Love is a song we all need to sing
to cure the cancer called hate.

Love is all about uniting everyone,
yet she will never dine at your table
with the gable of hate hanging from your plate.

Love is like the sunshine
that travels across time,
that each and every one can buy
even if you don't have a dime.

Take time
to embrace love.
Love is from above.

Let it adorn your heart
like pearls upon your neck.
Wear it for all to see.
When you do,
love will outlive hate.
Like the sand by the seashore,
learn to let love resize inside your heart.
Love.

Love, wonderful love,
the kind that comes only from above.
Bow your head, say a prayer
that we will find a way to light the torch of loving one another,
soaring on the wings of loving each other.
Hate cannot outlive love.
Love is a song we all need to sing
to cure the cancer called hate.

29

Pandemic of Hate

Have you not heard, I wonder?
What hole you have been hiding in?
The United States is having a verbal meltdown.
They have a new president, and he is draining the swamp,
he is building a wall with slime and lime
that will last a lifetime.
No one will be able to climb over his wall.

These days, a lot of people are talking from
both corners of their mouth.
It is as if they are having verbal diarrhea,
spreading germs in the middle of the midterms,
using terms of termination.
Leaving many to wonder how did we get to
this terminal of hate and division.
Have you not heard?
I wonder what hole you are hiding in.

This is a warning: those who have ears to hear and eyes to see,
You'd better look, listen, and learn.
The best is yet to come.
Beat your drum, blow your gum; it is time to run.

Many are buying more guns.
Where will you run
To get away from this pandemic of fear and division?

To add insult to injury, COVID-19 is on the loose like a wild goose
that no one can tame,
while politicians play the blame game
like a lame duck,
playing Duck, Duck, Goose.
The man-goose is on the loose.
Listen to the Iowa caucus howls;
many are licking the bowl.
If they are the proud ones
calling out to the boys
to come shovel the snow from off the streets decorating the street
with beetroot,
saying, Let the blood from the beets
hit the streets,
this is a warning: it's a new day dawning.

30

Remember

Remember when
remembering was fun,
when the sun would be beating on your chest?
Now you are being put to the test.

The journey you are on is long.
You long for better days
as you gaze back in time,
looking for happier times,
when life was simple.
You were always laughing,
showing your dimples,
with perfect teeth that were white,
as white as cotton.

Remember when you had no wrinkles,
And your freckles didn't bother you?
When you were carefree,
free from worrying?
Now, you worry about how to stop worrying people,
keep telling you that you must leave your troubles at Jesus's feet.

Remember when you could go to church
and leave the troubles of the world
at the front door
while you worship the father of life?
Not anymore.
Christians are too busy worshiping at the shrine of their earthly gods,
ganging up on those who refuse to worship their god.

Remember those three boys who were thrown into the fire
because they refused to worship the earthly god,
and when the God
they served showed up in the fire with them,
so the earthly god made a decree that everyone
must worship the God of those three boys?

Remember when life was simple,
and simpletons were not elected to the highest office of the land?
When people genuinely love from the heart,
when our hearts were burning
with love for each other?
We wouldn't want to hurt anyone or pluck out their eyes
just because we didn't see eye to eye.

Remember when God was God, and people used to depend upon him
for their daily bread?
But now our heads
are in the clouds of self-sufficiency,
of looking to an earthly god to sustain us.
Remember when remembering was fun?

31

Running Away

Running away,
running away,
trying to hide my pain,
pouring my emotions down the drain
while I rack my brain,
searching for the answers
to a question without answer.

Running away,
running away,
trying to hide behind a happy song,
singing instead of crying
because I'm too afraid to cry.
If I start crying,
I may not be able to stop my tears from falling
that I should have shed a long time ago.

Running away,
running away.
At times I feel like
I just wanted to lay down and die.
Please don't ask me why.

I am running,

running away

from a broken heart.

Sometimes in the middle of the night,

I hear her voice calling me, saying, "Mum, Mum,"

But before I can answer her,

I wake up shaking like a leaf in the part of a tornado.

Running away,

running away

from the sadness my heart is forcing me to feel.

At the door of my heart,

I erect a wall

that I used to dry up my tears,

Because I am afraid if I start crying,

I will not be able to stop.

Running away,

running away

from all this pain.

You may ask, What can I gain?

I keep asking myself again

and again.

Don't want to let down my guard.

That is why

I am running away,

running away,

because I cannot stand the pain.

32

The Have and the Have-Nots

The haves and the have-nots—
what do they have in common?
Do they share a common bond
that is stronger than Gorilla Glue?

The haves like to think
that they have what they have
because they are clever.
They learn how to use a meat cleaver
to shave off the dripping from the pocket of the haves-not.
The haves keep filling their pockets
with the sweat, blood, and tears
from the have-nots.

The have-nots are the ones who are bearing the heat of the hot sun,
working overtime all the time just to make ends meet,
to put meat on the table, and maybe vegetable.

The haves and the have-nots
don't see eye to eye.
The haves are of the opinion
that the have-nots

don't have just because they are too lazy to work,
saying that they are like leeches trying
to grab handouts.
That is all the have-nots are all about,
they say.
You will hear some educated fools
talking from both corners of their mouths,
behaving like Cruella de Vil,
dividing up the people in classes
in order for the haves
to afford to wear mink coats
and eat goat cheese,
trying to put a spell
in the minds of the have-nots,
turning them against each other,
saying that they have not
just because they are too lazy
to hold down a job,
jabbing at them with knives,
ready to cut down their children.
Holding them back from rising above the poverty of the mind,
even as they continue
to use them to dig coal mines
from the beginning of time.
Lining their pockets with the substance of the needy,
acting greedy,
like a king who doesn't care about anything
but himself and only himself.

Have-nots
are not rats.

Let them out of your traps.
Quit trampling on them.
They are not your personal trampoline.
Their lives matter too,
as a matter of fact.
I would really love to see you try to raise
a family on minimum wage.
Would you be able to sustain your glitz and glamor lifestyle?
I'm sure not!

Yes, Mr. and Mrs. Haves,
you would be like a blind dog
who has lost his tail,
roaming around in the dark.
How do you think you would feel
to have people throwing darts
at your eyes, trying to blind you to reality?

Sorry to break it to you,
Mr. and Mrs. Haves.
Half of what you have
belongs to the have-nots.

But of course,
you're all too greedy to understand.
Let me guess:
you are too greedy to see
that you, my friend, helped to create the problem of the needy
by refusing to acknowledge
that without the have-nots,

your Crock-Pot
would crack.
Then you would not be able to slow-cook and
drain the blood of the have-not.

How do you justify the fact that you have
millions in your bank account,
and the people who work for you
to give you your millions,
they can't even afford
to send their children to college
even though some are working twelve hours per day?
And to think that you turn around and call them lazy.
My eyes must be hazy.

Haves and have-nots—
what do they have in common?
They both breathe in the same air.

They will eventually die,
and their bodies will return to the dust
from which it came.
And yes,
they will meet again in hell
or in heaven.

33

Beauty of All

Oh, that we could comprehend
the awesome work that God has done,
the beauty and majesty of his creation,
the open heaven,
the rolling hills,
rivers that runs so wild
no one can tame them.

Have you ever stopped
to wonder how the stars
stay into orbit,
and why rabbits
like to eat carrots?

Do you ever stop
to think about the reason
why gold is called carats?
Can you tell me why you can train a parrot,
And if you pour grease down the kitchen sink,
your sink will clog up,
and you may have to pay big bucks to fix it?

Oh! that we all could find a way
to love each other,
put aside our differences,
get off the offense,
and stand back.

Cutting back on the insults
would result in harmony and peace.
Don't you think the war would cease,
and love for each other would increase?

If we could only come to the awareness
that God created the heavens and the earth,
but he created us in his lightness
so we can achieve greatness.
Oh! that we would comprehend
the awesome work that God has made.
Maybe we will stop and give him our praises.

34

The Law

To some, the law is lawless.
They help to create some of the mess
by messing with innocent children.
Why do you feel that you have to protect the country from babies
who can't even speak?

Many give speeches in the name of speeches,
even as the rich and famous.
TikToking out on the beaches
with the wealth of the poor.
They are still not satisfied with all they have taken out.
They are coming for more.

Who needs the law
if all they do is break the jaws
to talk and even sing
of the weeping mothers and hungry children?

How long will you be able to act like a monkey with a wrench,
trying to fix something that you have broken,
while embracing the fox
you call your personal friends?

Why do you cover your head with fake dreadlocks?

To some, the law is lawless.

What do you have to say?

Why not leave it to the naysayers to speak?

The law is bittersweet; the street has become the Wild West.

Should we be wearing bulletproof vests?

35

This Is a Warning

Leaving many wondering, How did we get to
this terminal of hate and division?

This is a warning:
ye who have ears to hear
and eyes to see,
look, listen, and learn.
The best of the worst is yet to come.
Beat your drums,
blow your gum.
It is time to hum.

Many are reaching for their guns.
Where will you run
to get away from this pandemic?

This is a warning:
the writing is on the wall.
Whom will you call?
If you have ears to hear,
you'd better listen and learn.

This has nothing to do
with the mark of the beast.

It is about the greedy
trying to feast on the flesh of the needy,
using the Bible as a crutch to stand on
as an excuse
to crush the will of the people.
Let Pinocchio tell it like no one else,
with his nose stretching across the entire world,
trying to crush the bones of the people showing his hand.
Still, many cannot read his play.
He keeps mingling in anything and everything,
blaming the fake media for his nose getting so long.

This is a warning:
ye who have ears to hear,
you'd better listen and learn.
We are at a point of no return.
Many are hitching a ride on his nose.
He is taking them to the heights that they have never reached before.
Some of them are beginning to build skyscrapers
in the cloud called confusion.

Like an illusionist, they have found a way to pause
the part of their brain that knows how to think
without thinkability.

There is only one reality: Swing on Pinocchio's nose,
never say no.

He is in charge; his minions follow his command.
If they don't, they get a call
from Ronnie tweets
or one of his aides: you are fired!

All of a sudden. you are like fried chicken.
sitting on the table of vegetarians.
No one wants you anymore.

This is a warning:
the one they call Pinocchio
will continue to rule with an iron fist
until the people understand that Pinocchio
is only a reflection of the heart of the nation.

Did you have sleepless nights,
when you learn about children being ripped from their mothers' arms
and put in the cages,
or when some people get killed?

Just because of the color of their skin,
Some things are left to be said.
If we don't talk about it, it will fade away.

Marcus Garvey got five years in prison
for trying to empower black people.
Maybe some will argue for a little stupidity
on his part, depending upon how you see it.

This is a warning.

Marcus Garvey was labeled a troublemaker.
After Marcus Garvey comes
Martin Luther King.
He too was killed, he was labeled a troublemaker.
And John Lewis
Tells us to get into good trouble.
Bill Clinton was impeached for you know what.

Jesus was killed for saying he was the Son of God,
for healing the sick
and feeding the hungry.
He went out of his way to heal women
and children.
He told us to feed the hungry
and clothe the naked.
Wait.
Did he say to rob the poor,
take away children from their mothers?
Jesus once said that anyone who hurts a child
would be better off putting a millstone
around his neck and drowning himself.

This is a warning:
unless we get to the place
where we start to examine our hearts
and start to confess to each other
that we did wrong,
things are going to get worse.

Are you a carrier of the pandemic of hate and division?

What will you do when a real pandemic hits you?
Please put down the luggage of hate;
it is not too late to partake
in the feast of love.

Climb down from the arms of the beast,
go ahead and feast at the table of peace.
This is warming:
stay away from the corner of disease and fear,
stop trying to change from the outside.

Real change begins from within.
This is a warning: ye who have ears to hear,
listen and learn,
stay away from the pandemic of hate.

36

Tomorrow

You can't make people happy.
Happiness comes from within.
What I have, let me freely give.

I will enter into his gate with thanksgiving,
into his courts with praise.
I will be thankful, I will bless your name.

As long as we live, there are always going to be problems.
Practice the power of praise,
preach the power of forgiveness.

Enjoy life as much as you can;
it is a gift that can be taken away without notice.
Please don't say, Tomorrow I will be happy.
Tomorrow I will show kindness.
Do it now.
Tomorrow, tomorrow—don't tell me about tomorrow.
Tomorrow is for liars and cheaters.
Tomorrow is a way of skipping today's responsibilities.

Tomorrow,
Tomorrow,
the mourners are standing by,
the gravediggers are busy digging your grave.
Tomorrow, tomorrow you will not be able
to hear them say dust to dust.
Tomorrow, tomorrow—what about today?
Dear heavenly Father, please help me today to stop
and give you thanks for today's blessings.

You can't make people happy.
Happiness comes from within.
What I have, let me freely give.

I will enter into his courts with thanksgiving,
Into his courts with praise.
I will be thankful to you, I will bless your name.

As long as we live, there are always going to be problems.
Practice the power of praise,
preach the power of forgiveness.

Enjoy life as much as you can;
it is a gift that can be taken away without notice.
Please don't say, Tomorrow I will be happy,
tomorrow I will show kindness.
Do it now.
Tomorrow, tomorrow—don't tell me about tomorrow.
Tomorrow is for liars and cheaters.
Tomorrow is a way of skipping today's responsibilities.

Tomorrow,

tomorrow.

The mourners are standing by.

The gravediggers are busy digging your grave.

Tomorrow,

tomorrow,

You will not be able to hear them say dust to dust.

Tomorrow,

tomorrow—

What about today?

Dear heavenly Father, please help me today

to stop and give you thanks for today.

37

When

When you get tired,
tired of living in a mental cage,
in the corner of self-pity,
feeling like an outcast,
wondering how long your life will last,
watching the world having a blast,
wondering what you should do.

Sometimes there's nothing.
You have to learn when to let go and let God
do the work in you and through you.
Turn the page over and allow
God to create something new in you,
or finish what he has already started.

Your life is not your own.
Your children really don't belong to you.
I know you refer to them as my children.
They are not yours.
Why don't you stop for a moment
and think about how you treat God's little pearls
that he has placed into your life?

It is time to step out of your mental cage,
time to engage
with the world.
Time to talk, time to hug your children, time to love them.
Time to teach them about the goodness of God.
It is time for you to stop feeling sorry for yourself.

Pick yourself from off the shelf,
save yourself from yourself.
When you're tired, take a rest and rest your
burden at the feet of the cross.

Down in your heart, you have a song.
Learn to sing your song,
your song of praise.
For this is the bridge that will keep you from
drowning in the chaos of everyday pain and sadness.

The beating and the banging of the drums
of distraction come in many ways.

The beeping of the messenger through daily messages,
trying to merge with your inner self,
preventing you from praying
and reading the word of God;
the ticking and the hissing of confusion,
doing everything to rob you of peace. Sometimes it echoes loud.

Sometimes it is the banging on the front door
that prevents you from praying or sleeping,
makes you wonder why everything is so chaotic.

Now you see why there are so many alcoholics:
they are too busy looking for comfort in the wrong places.
When you are tired of living in a mental cage,
my child learns to engage.
Place your troubles at the feet of the cross.

38

United Weight

United weight of fill in the blanks
while you walk the planks,
slicing plantains like Mr. Plankton
searching for the Krusty Krabs in Bikini Bottom,
expected to get out without any charges

United weight of fill in the blanks, take a stand.
Have you ever heard about quicksand?
Listen to Sandy the Siren from Texas.
We are being roasted.
Soon they will be slicing us up
like Texas toast, serving our blood
like red wine
while they commit crimes
of having no spine.

United weight of fill in the blanks,
we are all walking the planks.
Many are wondering if this is a prank.
Can I be frank?
This is what happens when a punk

is in charge of deciding,
to decide on what is best for he himself and only him.

United weight of fill in the blanks.
like Frank Sinatra said, regrets, he had a few.
But best of all, he did it his way.
This is our lot;
the rest of the world is laughing.
We are the ones who love to poke our noses
into everyone business.

United weight of fill in the blanks.
Our own children
tried to burn down the house of the people.
Or maybe I should say
they were about to paint
the house with blood.
The blood of their brothers and sisters
in the name of proving a point,
to show their loyalty to you-know-who.

Now, many are saying
that they shouldn't be charged
because they were only doing
what they have been told.

Wonder what message they will be sending
to the black sheep in the family
who are familiar with getting tased
and shot just for standing on the sidewalk,

holding up a BLM sign
on the street of liberty and justice for all.

Michael Vick must be having a fit.
He was stripped of the right to play football
until he did his made up time
for his crime.

Have anything to say about you,
who used the bully pulpit to destroy Kaepernick
just because he decided to take a knee in protest
of injustice toward black people?
Many were outraged. How dare Kaepernick disrespect
the flag of the United weight of fill in the blanks.

They throw him over the plank.
You whip him all the way to the bank.
He was shank
because he couldn't climb up the rank
of forgetting about his black brothers and sisters
who are still being treated like
second-class citizens.

The world watches the handling
of those who were marching
for George Floyd, who was murdered in the street
by a police officer who was been paid by taxpayers.

When Black Lives Matter
marched in protest of the killing of Mr. Floyd,
the players of hate and hostility.

They thought it was okay watching a police officer
pushing down an old man on his head,
sending him to the hospital
bleeding from his nose.

Some are of the opinion
that the folks who took part in standing up
for the Black Lives Matter movement
are anti-American.
But now these same people are saying
that the folks who stormed the capital building
must not face any consequence,
even though they were trying
to paint the capital building with
the blood of Mike Pence.

The people in power
with the power for the hour
seem to be willing to cover
their hands with blood to hang Mike Pence
in the name of keeping the piece of history that
they never want to give up: power.
The grim reaper is okay with putting his hands
under the bench of defending the claws
in the law that was meant to keep black folks in their place,

while the rest of the world is watching to see what
the United weight of fill in the blanks
is going to do to make sure nothing like this happens again.

If nothing is done, our children are the ones
Who will be walking the planks,
wondering if this is a prank.

The leadership of this country
needs a really good spanking.
Better yet, they need a BMW.
United States of America, where did you go wrong?

America, are you saying
it is okay to kill our police officers?
Who is doing
what we are paying them to do?
And remind me again what Mike Pence's crime was,
why he was given the death penalty.
Who gave the order to hang him?

United weight of America fills in the blanks,
the leaders of this country need a good spanking.

Better yet,
They need a good BMW:
a black mama's whooping.

39

I Know Who I Am

I know who I am.
I need no reminder.
How can I forget when I live in a world of
white is always right and righteous?
In a world where a black woman is reminded of slavery,
and the stigma of blackness every day?

I know who I am.
I have no ill will against
a white righteous woman,
where the only thing she has
going on for her is her whiteness.
Because you are white,
you think you have the right
to try to control my life?

I know you may not believe me
when I tell you
that I am not mad at you.
You can date whomever you want.
If the truth should be told, I'm glad you're dating him.
I am really happy for you.

You can have the gold,
or should I say fool's gold.

You know what I can't understand?
Why do you feel your whiteness
gives you the right to spit on my blackness,
telling me how to raise my children?

Trying to buy their affection with your rotten intentions.

I know how to read between the lines.
Your plan is to get me all worked up,
to get under my skin
in order to skin me.
But I'm not going to let you make me sin.

This black woman has a backbone.
I am not afraid of you.
I will fight,
but I fight with dignity.
I do not roll in the mud; I fight with my intellect.
I'm ahead of your game.

My ancestors, the strong black women,
like the woman they call Moses,
who run the underground railroad
to help to free runaway slaves.

Rosa Parks, who parked her black
backside on the seat on the bus,

refusing to give it up to a white person.
I have some of her spirit.

I know when to fight
and when to let go.
It doesn't mean that I don't have strength,
because I refuse to fight
and get down on your level.

I am a level-headed woman.
I'm going to be okay.
Do whatever you want,
because I know who I am.

40

Victim of the System

Inspired by Social Issues

When I was born, my mother and father
loved me beyond the moon and the stars.
I was their sunshine,
I was the happiest kid in the world.
Then something happened, and it changed my parents.
They stopped hugging each other and started yelling at each other.
Then one day, they quit hugging me,

My dad lost his job.
It was hard for my mom to get a good paying job
because she had dropped out of school when she was sixteen years old,
because she was pregnant with me;
Her parents kicked her out because she got pregnant with me.
I keep thinking that everything is my fault.

I know within my heart that when I was born,
my parents loved me.
How would I know that they love me?
I see photos of me hanging on the wall, and on their phones.

I am only a child.
I cannot tell you what is wrong with my parents,
but I know that something is wrong with them.

One day, I told my teacher
that my parents need help.
Next thing I know, DHS was at my front door.
They took me away from my parents,
saying that they were unfit parents.

I told them that we used to ride our bikes around the block,
and went swimming,
but they don't want to listen to me.

Next thing I know,
I was standing before a judge,
and my parents were standing across from me.
I wanted was to hug them,
but they didn't let me.
This is all my fault.
If I had not told my teacher
that something was wrong with my parents,
none of this would have happen.

I now have foster parents, and a foster sister and brothers.
I don't need foster parents.
I want my own parents,
because I know that they love me,
and buy me birthday presents.

One day, I yell at my foster mom,
telling her that I hate her.
That earned me a slap across the face
and a long timeout in the bathroom,
sitting on the floor in the dark.

Now, I have no one to talk to about what is happening to me.
I have no teacher, because I am home-schooled.
Whenever I act out, they punish me by withholding my food.

Because I was always acting up, I got less and less food,
and more and more beatings.
They would sit in front of me and eat.

It got to the point that I never really wanted to eat.
I was hoping that if I got sick enough,
they would have to take me to the hospital.
Then I would make a run for it to save my life,
And then the police would find me.
Then I would get a chance to tell them how bad they were treating me.

They never took me to the doctor.
I felt like I was just a ghost.
Then one day, I became a ghost!
Yes! I died.
Yes, I am speaking from the grave,
to all the people who have let me down.

My foster parents by now are in jail, where they belong.
I would still be alive if the system was better
at how they vet foster parents.

They took the money you gave them to care
for me and enrich themselves.
I am a victim of the system that was meant to protect me!
But I starved to death while they get to live.

I was a victim of the system.
My parents were victims.
They have to live with the guilt of
having their child taken away from them.

My parents suffered from depression, and they are not the only ones.
What DHS fails to understand was
that my parents loved me more
than any foster parent ever could.

Here's what I want to find out:
if everyone had my best interest at heart,
like they told me when the judge deemed my parents unfit,
how come none of them came
to my rescue at my foster parents' house,
where I was beaten, raped, and starved?
But now that I am dead, everyone starts to care.
I don't care anymore.
I was a victim of the system.

It's too late to help me.
However, you can help others from reliving my nightmares.

Please try harder to help parents become better parents.
Don't allow them to become victims of the system.

41

Well of Evil

Are you still drinking from the well of hate and evil?
Are you still hungry for more blood?
Bob Marley said it well:
many more will have to suffer,
many more will have to die.
Is anyone even asking why?

A dark cloud of hate is drifting across the nation,
a thick, dark cloud call hate and division.

Where are the missionaries of peace and love,
the kind of love that comes from above?

Stop drinking from well of evil; the veil is ripped apart.
A spirit of hate and fear climbed aboard in the hearts of people
who are trying to change the color of the nation.
They are retaliating against the maker of the human race.

It is a disgrace to think that self-made god
is trying to change the face of God,
embracing evil in the name of a righteous God.

Are you still too blind to see what's going on?
It is just a matter of time before the United States
will step back into the days of caveman mentality.

This is a sad reality.
Stop drinking from the well of hate.

Can't you see that we are hemorrhaging?
It is not too late
to clean the slate.

Apply the brake of understanding.
Stop drinking from the well of hate and evil.

Part 2

42

For the Sake of My Sanity (Part 2)

For the sake of my sanity,
I have to deal with my reality.
Most times I feel like I am about to lose my mind.

I have been depressed for a very long time.
I have to find a way to rise
above the deep feeling of depression.

I am not a child anymore,
even though It feels like I am trapped
inside my youth.
That being said,
I have to find a way to tell my truth,
if only to clear my head.

Tired of lying awake in bed at nights,
worrying about my life,
and hiding from the past.

I was of the impression that I was over
what had happened to me
when I was a little girl.

How can it be that I still drive around with it
in my heart like a sharp knife?
My heart is getting old.
If I don't find a way to unload my feelings,
I am afraid that I may die before my time.

I wanted so much out of life
when I was still a little girl.

I yearned for my mother's love and acceptance.
I felt like I was nothing.
My life meant nothing to others,
even though I knew that my grandmother loved me very much.

Knowing how much she loves me
was why I was not able to tell her what had happened to me.
I had no one to talk to; I never heard anyone talk about sex.
We never asked where babies came from.
Sex education was not a topic in school,
unlike now,
and of course we didn't have the internet.
There was no Me Too movement.

I listened to politicians
talk about women and girls
who said that they have been raped
as if we are dirty liars who deserve to burn in hell.
You know to stay away from strangers,
but no one taught you how to avoid familiar foes.

Do you even have any idea how hard it has been
for me to carry the guilt and shame?
Not to mention blaming myself.
Can you even begin to understand
how I feel about myself
when I can't even remember how old I was when I lost my virginity?

Was it the first time it had happened to me,
or was it that it was the first time
I knew about it?

My mom was living in another country.
We never had a telephone,
so I was not able to reach her.
I had this terrible fear of my rapist.
If I had told anyone,
would he have tried to kill me?

Something within me kept telling me
that if you want to stay alive,
you'd better keep your mouth shut

To hide my secret, I became an adult in a child's body.
My mind worked overtime trying to protect
myself by hiding my emotion.

It is only by the grace of God
that I have not lost my sanity.
There, I was a little girl,
thinking about how to protect my unborn children.

A little girl should never have to be worrying about her unborn,
feeling like a reject that no one seems to want.

Today, I am going to church.
I am making myself go.
I have not been going to church.
It's not that I don't love God.
It is because
church reminds me of happier times,
and I am still lost in time.

God is telling me to open up about my struggles,
but I have been running away from the call.
How can I,
how will I,
begin to really be unmasked?

When will I be able to clear the fog in my mind?
I talked with my dad yesterday.
He is a tower of strength to me.
I told him about a week ago about what happened to me.
It was so hard to open up to him,
and I started to feel so dirty.

Don't even want to talk to him anymore.
I am still learning how to cope.

Not able to understand why I am feeling like an outcast,
wondering how long my life will last.

I kept telling myself
that the feelings of shame and condemnation would pass.

I was wrong.
It will not go away on its own.
My dad was supportive.
He told me he was sorry he was not there to protect me
when I needed him.
He said that I must find a way to talk about my
feelings if I don't it will make me sick.

He is right: my arm has been hurting and tingling.
Funny how our bodies work.
For many, many years, I masked my pain.
Now it seems that my heart is running out of space.

I am beginning to feel anxiety pains; it is now getting worse.
Thanks to all the talk on TV about these women who have been raped
and are just coming out after so many years.

I realized that I too have to heal.
Hiding behind a song will not heal my battered emotion.
It is time for me to open up about everything.
You can't heal if you don't feel.

With a heavy heart,
I have decided to write about my pain and suffering.
I cannot hide it any longer;
there is nowhere to hide.

Every heart knows its own pain.
You have to open up your wounds
and let the pus drain out.

The best way to do that is to forgive the ones who have hurt you.
Then use your painful past to help someone deal with their own pain.

That is why I am opening up the window to my heart
And cleaning myself off, so I can move on.
I know that it is going to be hard.

I know without a shadow of a doubt that I
have to come to grips with my past.

If I want to stay alive and not get a brain tumor,
I can't have my brain on overdrive anymore.
That is why I have decided to write about
my years of being traumatized,
of carrying around the secret of sexual abuse.

I am not trying to get attention.
I am simply trying to help someone
who maybe going through what I have been through,

to help them understand that the
only way to heal
is to allow yourself to feel the pain.
You cannot hide from reality.

It is what it is.

The hole inside your heart gets deeper and wider every day.

Speak up—you are not alone.

The only way to heal is to expose

the demons of molestation and rape for what they are.

Yes! For the sake of my sanity, I am learning to speak up,

not so much for myself

but for someone who is too weak to speak up.

You are not alone.

Someone will believe you.

For the sake of your own sanity,

stop blaming yourself.

43

Who Are You?

Who are you to judge me,
to tell me who to be
and not to be?

Why are you so busy
interfering in my affairs?
My life is not a fairytale.

I have much to fear,
however I choose to
walk past my fears.

I am not looking back.
Whatever you have to say to me,
have the balls to look me in the eyes
and tell me what you have to say to my face.

Who are you to keep on
belittling me,
making me out to be a monster
without feelings,

when you have no way
of really understanding what makes me tick?

You are like a tick
on my back,
slowly draining my blood.
Are you not tired?
Tired of swimming in my blood?
Who are you to judge me?

44

I Heard through the Grapevine

I heard it through the grapevine
that children are growing up too fast.
Childhood doesn't last long anymore.
The world is at their fingertips.
They don't even have to leave home to take a trip into the unknown,
where perverts dress like children eating chicken nuggets,
fooling our children,
selling drugs and guns to young children
in the name of love and freedom.

Mothers are under pressure,
left with the burden of parenthood.
Some are bringing strange men into their beds
Just to keep food on the table,
wearing the label of shame.

I heard it through the grapevine
that many fathers are more interested
in themselves and only themselves.

They really don't care
if their children go to bed hungry.

They are in a hurry,
trying to fool the next woman
who is looking for a new
lover and a father,
the father they never had.

I heard it through the grapevine
that many mothers are on their own, struggling
to feed their hungry children,
struggling to make ends meet,
wondering how they are going to feed their children,
while some preachers and politicians
are reminding us that abortion is a sin,
forgetting about the sin
of not obeying God's word
to feed the hungry.

Look out for the orphans and the widows.
These days, it is the single mothers
who are playing the part of widowhood,
not to mention the fathers,
who are gun down by lawmen
in the name of keeping a piece of peace.

I heard it through the grapevine
that when the pandemic hit, it didn't care about race or creed.
If you are greedy or needy,
it will knock on your door,
leaving you holding on to sorrow
with no hope for tomorrow.

Lord, please provide for the single
mothers and fathers who are trying to be
both mothers and fathers to their children
in this season of COVID-19.

Whereas the rich can stay home,
the working poor are getting poorer
while the leaders drag their feet
as to when to sign a relief bill.

The rich are chilling, grilling, and sipping champagne,
expecting the poor to clean up after them.

Some rich folks are trying to buy up the vaccines.
Some care more about making sure that their dogs get rabies shots
than the children whose parents are the working poor.
Some are worried about if they are going to catch COVID-19.
Some have nothing to eat and no water to take a shower.

The rich and powerful
have time to tweet on the hour
about how tormented they are,
having to stay home in their mansions,
Making millions on the stock market,
forgetting about the single mothers
who are working in the supermarket.
The rich are busy fulfilling their online orders
so they can stay home and complain about being bored.

I heard in through the grapevine
that the little, that the poor, will have to be taken away.

45

Who Do You Think?

So who do you think I am?
I am not your fool anymore.
I am brave, I am bold.
My truth will be told.
I am not afraid of you anymore.
For all these years, I have allowed you to torment me.
No more!
I will rise,
I will speak up,
I will tell the world.
I am not afraid anymore.

It was not my fault.
I was just a child;
I did not know right from wrong.
I refuse to suffer in silence anymore.
We all have to find a way to expose sexual abuse for what it is.

We may be able to stop it
if we learn to speak up about it.

The trauma would not be so bad.
Look at me: I am brave, I have survived the trauma of sexual abuse.

I am strong. You are strong.
Together, we are stronger.
We will hold hands and tell the world that we refuse to be victims.

We refuse to be victims.

You will never be able to understand
what we have been through.
So go ahead, sit in your high chair, looking
down on us as troublemakers.
It is your quest to stop us from becoming
who we were meant to be.
We are not victims anymore.
We are overcomers.

I will survive, we will survive.
We tell our story so others can get strength
to heal from the trauma of sexual abuse in all forms.
Who do you think you are?
You can't control me anymore.
I am free from the guilt.
You cannot play me like a guitar anymore.

46

Does Ape Vape?

Do apes like to vape?
Or do they just spend all day scraping their
brains through their noses,
wondering, How did Moses cross the Red Sea without a boat?
Wonder what was floating inside his head.
Could that be the reason why some people stay in bed
with an empty head, with too much food floating in their belly?
While I dream of drinking jelly coconut water,
watching politicians promise change.
Instead, they're handing out chains of
disillusion, disorder, and divisions,
trying to come to a conclusion about collusion.
Sounds like delusion to me.

Wondering why apes can communicate with each other,
and why humans spend too much time talking online
to people with fake names
to stay in the game of modern-day vibes.
Vaping and talking about presidential vice peeps, trying
to make up their mind as to who to vote for.

If apes could vote or vape,
what brand vape would they use?
Who would they vote for?
Probably a banana republic.

Who would you vote for
if apes could vape?
Gives you something to think about
the next time you light up.

47

What If?

What if today should be my last day on Earth?
What if life as I know it
is about to change into what I don't know?

What if the boy with the black skin you shot and killed
had the cure for cancer,
and he is not really a gangster?
What if God is split in the middle,
half black and half white?
Would you love him any less?

What if the children should become the parents,
and the parents turn into children?
Should they treat us just like we treat them?
What if the world was not round, and there
was no black and brown people?
Would that make the world a better place?

What if preachers should start practicing what they preach?
What if the sun refuses to shine, and we become lost in time?

What if before you become the president
of the United States of America,
instead of showing your tax returns,
you have to walk a day in the shoes of the poorest
person without protection of your bodyguards?

What if politicians were only paid ten dollars an hour, or maybe seven,
and were told that the taxpayers should not be
allowed to pay for their health insurance?
Would they call in sick, or would they lead with a big stick?

What if we show kindness instead of talking about it?
What if Christianity is really about humanity and
the way to heaven is going through hell?

What if life is a well of wisdom that you have
to draw understanding from?

What if love was the air we breathe,
and our hearts were a reservoir filled with peace?
Do you think the killing would cease?

What if tomorrow, when you wake up and look into the mirror,
you're wearing the face of the person you don't like,
and that person wakes up with your face and the desires of your heart?
Would that make you fear for your life?
What if today should be our last day on Earth,
because for some of us, it will?

What if, in getting ready to die, we are only
getting ready to start living?

What if today is all we've got,
and yesterday will judge us?
Would we be proud of what we have accomplished?
Did we spend too much time watching garbage and TV
while allowing our hearts to become a place to collect rubbish?

What if your life is an open book,
and everyone is free to take a look?
What would they see?
What if motherhood is just a fleeting moment,
and the tears we shed will only be for a moment?
Would we spend time loving and hugging our children?

What if today should be our last dinner around the table of life?
Would we have made peace with the ones we love
while forgiving the ones who hurts us?

48

Baby

Baby, I never meant to single you out,
but I had to.
I had no choice because if I don't speak up with the only voice I have,
my existence will be meaningless.

Baby, I didn't mean to have to beat my chest
and confess to knowingly giving up my rights
just so you can love me.

Baby, I need you to love me,
But not at the expense of me stop loving myself
in order for you to love me.

I'm not going to be a zero
just so you can be a hero.

Baby, why are you accusing me of being mean to you?
Just because I refuse to let you take away my self-worth?

Your reputation is on the line,
but my life is hanging in the balance.

Maybe by now, you should have realized
that I have grown up, I'm no longer your toy.

Maybe you still expect me to treat you
like you are good while pretending that I am the devil,
splitting your head while injecting you with evil thoughts,
serving you a broth of evil intentions.

Maybe you really don't know how
or when to stop massaging your own fragile ego.

Honey, this hero refuses to let you continue the treat her like zero.
Baby, it is time to say goodbye.

49

The Load I Carry

Ihave been carrying around a spirit of
rejection.
This is a heavy load to drag around.
One may ask, Why not just dump it off somewhere?
Easier said than done.

When you are from a culture that doesn't talk
about things openly with children,
don't expect that child or children to be able to just talk
about things that are hurting them with just anyone.
Not even when they get older.

Shame is like a garment that some people wear.
Until you find a way to get new clothes to wear,
you are not going to undress for the world to see all your nakedness.
For me, I have been hurt so many times;
that is why I make it my quest not to hurt anyone if I can help it.

I am not talking about letting people walk all over me
for the sake of having them like me. That was a long time ago.
I always tell myself that I don't know what people are going through,
so I never want to be the one to add to their pain.

I see myself telling my life story.
However, I managed to convince myself
that no one cared enough to listen to what I have to say.

Maybe I am right, maybe I wrong. However,
I will still tell part of my story.
No one really tells everything.
Funny how things happen in the life of a person.
When you find yourself self on the hard knocks of life,
you either sink or rise.
I choose to rise.
For the sake of myself, I have to rise
above the pain and sufferings.
All my children are almost able to take care of themselves,
so if I only live through their eyes, what will I do in
eight years, when my youngest turns eighteen?

At my age, I have to find a way to rise above
what people did to me or did not do for me.

I am strong even though most times, I don't feel that way.
My greatest fear is that I will be rejected.
It is hard to understand why I feel this way.

I don't know if it has anything to do with the fact that
I had no one to tell me I was doing good as a child.

I am a good mother. I have given of myself to my children
much more than I got from my parents.
At times I cry, wondering what my life would have been
if my parent did for me what I have done for my children.

I am not blaming them; they did what they could.
I could be somebody, yet here I am,
a nobody still trying to be somebody.
My oldest sister once told me that God gave us the parents we needed.

If I had parents who were able to give me emotional stability,
I would never gained the ability to step into my
creativity of painting word pictures,
or walking into a room and feeling the anxiety
of the person lying in a hospital bed.

If the truth should be told,
all I ever wanted was to have a place to call home.
In my mind, I wanted to make sure that my children never
have to move from one place to the next like I did.

But when you are poor and don't have power and might,
and your grandmother raised you to know that stealing is wrong,
you have to work for what you want.
You refuse to steal or beg.
That is why it makes me mad
when I look around me and see people who steal from others
just so they can pretend that they have something.
Don't they know that when they rob the poor,
they are stealing from God?

I am aware that I have no power to change the world.
I am learning to rearrange my internal world right now.
I am sitting on the edge,
trying to maintain my sanity,

because all I ever wanted out of life
was to be a good mother.

Now, I find myself running away,
trying to shield myself from the memories of my daughter.
Can't seems to come to grips of her lying alone in a dark, cold grave.

I am trying to be brave.
Sometimes I wish that I was the one in the grave.
When will the pain subside?
For now, I am beside myself with grief.
This is why I write: to find relief.

Believe me when I tell you
all I ever wanted out of life was to be a good mother.
The load I am carrying is not mine to carry.
Lord, please take these feelings from me.

50

When Did It Begin?

When did it begin?
When will it end?
Who is willing to pin the tail on the donkey,
the donkey of racism?
The next time you are made to feel like
you have more rights than your brothers or sisters
whose skin and hair look different from yours,
ask yourself, How much input did you have
in choosing who your parents were?

When did it begin?
When will it end?
If you could find a way to eradicate
from the face of the earth
the people you call invaders and rodents,
would that make you love yourself more?

Would it make God love you any more?
Why do you hate yourself so much?

When did you start hating yourself?
When will you start loving yourself?

And don't you tell me that you love God,
because I'm not the one who came up with this saying
that if you can't love your brothers and sisters from all tribes,
you cannot love God.

Stop hating in the name of God.
Stop killing in the name of God.

Who is going to pin the tail on the donkey,
the donkey they call racism?
When did it begin, and when will it end?
Will it ever end?

51

What Is Courage?

What is courage? Some may ask.
Why do we need it?
You cannot really say you have courage
until you are faced with some form of danger,
when someone you love is depending on you
to help them out of a predicament.

If you are brave,
you will uproot the spirit of fear
and grab onto the arm of courage
to find a way to pull that person out of their distress.

Courage is knowing what to do
when you are feeling fearful.
Courage is not the absence of fear;
yet it will not look away,
it will stare danger in the eyes
and find the strength to do the impossible
when everyone else says it is impossible.
What is courage?
Courage is not the absence of fear.

52

Love Never Dies

Love never dies.
It may fall asleep
like flowers in the snow.
You need to know that as soon as the sun
comes shining through, melting the snow,
love will bloom again.

Love never dies,
even if you tried to hide or lie
about the way you feel.

You can't hide love; it comes from above
like a turtle dove.
Love will find you
even if you try to hide in the basement
of a broken heart.

Love never dies.
It goes beyond the confusion.
It will sweep you off your feet
and cover you while you sleep on your bed.

Love is a voice in your head,
telling you to let go of your fears.
Time to give in to love.
Love will fall asleep, but love never dies.

53

Wake Up! Wake Up!

Inspired by Social Issues

Wake up, America!
Wake up, America!
Shake up, America!
Stop pretending that you can't see.
Stop pretending that you can't hear.
What is going on?

What are you carrying in your backpack?
Saying and doing are two different things.
Any coward can read a written speech.

You need backbone to stand up to racism.
Stop the *-ism* and the schism.

Why are you skimming the truth?
give us the whole truth and nothing but the truth.

Wake up, America!
Speak up, America!
Don't be a pig wearing lipstick,

waiting for the next mud hole,
before pushing back on hate and division.
We need a new vision,
a vision
of what it means to be kind to our brothers and sisters.

Wake up, America!
Speak up, America!
Shake up, America!
How long will you continue to shed innocent blood?
How long?
Tell me how long
before you will have another mass shooting.
How long?

Wake up, America!
Speak up, America!
Shake up, America!
Hate and bitterness
are leading us down the pathway of blindness
toward hate and injustice

while some stand on the sidelines
smoking their pipe of indifference.

It is time for us to make a difference.
Forget the word *indifference*—
we all bleed red blood.

Stop throwing raw meat to the base.
Spread the table of kindness.

Put roses in a vase.
Time to change the fragrance in the room.
Wake up, America!
Speak up, America!
Shake up, America!

The sleeping giant has awoken.
Can't you hear the roar of the mighty giant?

Goliath is standing on top of the mountain,
looking down on his minions.
They shake at his mighty roar.
Goliath!
Goliath!
It is blowing like a hurricane,
whistling like the wind,
coming through the window pane.

The mountains shake,
and the people tremble with fear.
The children line up in fear, wondering if anyone really cares.
Meanwhile, mothers shed tears of helplessness
even as they scrape up the flesh
of their children off the streets.
Bitterness sweeps
across the country, spreading like wildfire.

The giant has awoken;
Many words are spoken.
First it was a drip, drip, drip.
Now it is pouring out of the mouth of elected officials,

making it official
to hate people who do not look a certain way.
The giant has awoken.
Wake up, America!
Speak up, America!
Shake up, America!
If you don't, your streets are going to be paved with innocent blood.
Not just black and brown blood,
But white blood too,
if there is such a thing as white blood.
Wake up, America!
Speak up, America!

This collusion is going to lead to a collision.
Not everyone can see the vision.

You may not want to hear what I have to say,
but you'd better listen to every word I say.
This collusion is about to start a revolution.

If you don't believe me, you'd better go read the book of Revelation.

This collusion is about to start a war that only God himself can finish.

It sounds fishy.
Prophecy is fulfilling.
The antichrist is marching to the invisible drums.

The yardstick of iniquity is poking at your conscience,
telling you to take heed,
but you refuse to heed the call.
Wake up, America!
Speak up, America!

54

We Don't Know

We don't know what is going on.
What is wrong with the minds of the people doing the killing?
Are they suffering from lack of sunshine,
or the lack of love for humanity?
Why do we move from one calamity to the next?

You don't know if gun control will stop the senseless killings.
Part of listening to the chilling cries of weeping mothers
trying to scrape their children's brains off the street.
We don't know when the senseless killings will end,
or if they will ever end.
Should we just stop watching the news?

Put our minds on cruise control to hide our scars
from the callousness of the haters of peace.

Who is doing the killings?
We don't know what to do—
or don't we?

Everybody want to talk about gun rights,
second amendments rights,

the right to bear arms.
Does that give you the right to shoot off somebody else's arm
with your firearm?

Frankly, I am sick and tired
of listening to people sending sympathy and prayers.

When children get gunned down in their classroom,
I am still asking,
When is enough going to be enough
to convince you that enough is enough?

America has the most school shootings,
the most gun violence in the world.
That is something that needs looking into.
Tell me, please,
why is America so hungry for blood?

We do not know what to do
to stop these senseless killings—
or do we?

55

Just Smile

The most important thing to me is a smile.
Read my writing on the board:
the most important thing you can do for me
is to smile.
I don't need your money.
I don't need your pity.
All I need is a genuine smile.

Your smile
can brighten up an old man's heart
who is about to die.
If you live to be old, as old as I am,
only then will you understand
what it means to an old man
to see someone
smile from the heart.

Yes! the most important thing to me
is to get a genuine smile,
and you gave that to me. Thank you.

56

To-Go List

Who is on the to-go list?
The hammer or him, him or her?
Do what I tell you
to do.

When I tell you
what to do,
this is my house!
My rules!
I call the shots!
I own all of you!
You are my coin-slot-operated machines.
They call me crude.
Some say I don't have a clue.
But I do what I do
because I know what I'm doing.

Who is on the to-go list?
Say what you want.
I'm going to do what I want.

From I was a child, I got what I wanted.
No one ever said no to me.

I know how to win.
Some say I am just a kid
looking for attention.

All I care about is
what I am all about.
So call me crude, rude.
Frankly, I don't give a damn.
My name is not Saddam.
Who is on the to-go list?
When I hit, I don't miss.

Don't you dare test me.
If you don't listen to what I tell you,
you will be on the to-go list.

57

When Heaven Speaks

When heaven speaks, let the earth rejoice.
Let the people you created
worship in your temple.

When heaven opens up its mouth,
let the birds sing songs of adoration.
When the river is racing,
racing to meet the ocean,
and the lion roars,

and all the beasts of the field race
to get away from the avalanche of the snow.
They know that the snow is
a mighty, silent force
that can take them away
before you have a chance to run and hide from it.
When heavens speaks,
it teaches us to keep the peace,
to be silent so we can embrace
the tranquility

of listening to the birds
sing songs of melody.

When heavens speaks, we need to listen.
Okay?

58

Don't

Don't give in to the naysayers.
See yourself where you want to be.
Yesterday is gone;
today is yours.
Hold on with all your strength.
Don't give up.

Don't give in to the pressures of doing it right.
Just do your best and leave the rest.

Find a way to rest on the promises of hope and faith.
Don't give in to the naysayers,
who are standing at the root
of your tree with their axes,
trying to cut you down.
Bear your fruit.

Don't give in to them.
Bloom in the mud,
the muddy place where you find yourself.

Some of us are born into poverty; some are born into riches.

If you stop and reflect
upon what is going on inside your mind,
you will understand that Jesus, the Son of God,
was born on the wrong side of the tracks.

Whose side are you on?
Where do you belong?

Are you like water from a broken pipeline,
gliding aimlessly down the street of life,
searching for answers,
only to find yourself fallen in the gutters
of life chaos and confusion?

Whose side are you on?
Where are you? Where do you belong?
Do you even know where you are?
And why you are where you are,
my friend?

Don't give in to the naysayers.
See yourself where you want to be.
When you do, you will learn to accept yourself.

Then you will understand that naysayers won't have the last say.
Don't give in to the naysayers.

59

Garbage In

Garbage in the mind,
causes your brain to lag behind.
You need to find the courage to deal with all
that is going on inside your head.

When you put your head
on your pillow at nights,
does the light inside your head start to shine bright,
stopping you from falling asleep?

Garbage in your mind
will keep you up at nights.
Your blood pressure will rise.

So be wise and try to find a way to
unclog the clutter in your mind.

Garbage in the mind
causes your brain to malfunction.
Time to refocus,
teach your brain a new chorus.

60

Out of the Norm

Sometimes you just need to get away
from the stress and mess.
Take a little time to have a cup of tea,
forget about work-related stress,
let the children eat leftovers.

If you cannot take time for you,
no one will be able to help you.
So I am begging you:
find a way to destress from life's chaos.

Choose to be happy. You may not have the ideal life,
or anyone who loves you the way you think they should.
But as long as you learn how to love yourself and be kind to yourself,
you will be all right.

Take your jacket off, lay on the carpet,
turn off the TV, and take up a book and read.

Use your creativity, create your own creed.
Lavish yourself with the lotion of self-awareness.

You owe it to yourself to take the time to
listen to the music that is coming
from within your heart.

Get away from the tintinnabulation,
from the madness of everyday living.
Everyone is looking for something.
Most people take and take,
forgetting to give back,
turning their backs on the little pleasures of life.
Stick out your tongue, taste the snowflakes
as they silently fall from heaven.
Not a sound to be heard,
yet it lights up the earth with its brightness.

Get out of the norm.
Stop and give adoration
To the one who created the world.
Sometimes you just need to get away
and spend some time with yourself
to regain your strength.

61

How Do I?

For the sake of my sanity,
I need to climb over the bull in the room.
How do you rise above the hurt and the pain?
How do you maintain your composure in a world
that tells you that you don't belong in it?

How do you get past the sadness and loneliness
that linger at your front door?
You are screaming, Mayday! Mayday!

Yet many believe that you are enjoying your heyday,
so they look the other way.
For the sake of my sanity,
I have to find a way to climb over the bull in the room.

62

Why Don't You?

Why don't you meet with me right?
Where I am at, where might that be in the depths of despair,
in the dust of disappointment,
in the cornfield of regrets
as I wander on the streets of loneliness,
trying to cling to happiness?

Even as I undress the sadness
that is buried deep inside me from yesterdays,
following me around like a wounded dog
whose tail has been tied between its legs
and without a voice to bark.

Why don't you meet me where I am at? Sit with me. Let's talk.
No, this is not your turn to talk.
I need you to listen.

I get it: it's hard to listen to a person like me
who has a million things to unload.
You don't have the time to listen.

But more important, you don't have the room for my extra junk
because your trunk is already full of your own junk.

Why do you keep asking how I'm doing
when you know that you don't have the time
to listen to what I have to say?

Why don't you meet me right where I'm at?
In the middle of my sadness?

63

The Finisher

How to finish the race,
find a way to embrace the author and finisher of your faith?

Follow after peace; it will take you
through the valley of understanding.

While you are at the valley of understanding,
try to let your cup become full.
When you do, you will start to bear
the fruit of love.

How to finish the race, learn to be graceful even when
you are being beaten by the storms of life.

Bring your own lunch to the table of life.
Share your thoughts.
But most important, listen more than you speak.
Find a way to walk in love.

Any unity unites the spirit of brotherhood and sisterhood.

Let love live in the neighborhood.
Let's finish the race with love by our side.
That is how you finish the race
with grace and save face.

64

Love Is the Strongest Force

Love is strong; you cannot break
the bond of the stronghold called love.

Love is stronger than the wings of a turtle dove.
It flutters inside your heart, making you smile.

Love will never bow down to evil
or hide behind the veil of loving some and hating some.
Love will remain the same.
Love is a song we all need to sing
to cure the cancer called hate.

Love is all about uniting everyone,
yet she will never dine at your table
while the gable of hate is hanging from your plate.

Love is the sunshine that travels across time
And that reaches each and every one.

Everyone can buy love even if they don't have a dime.

Take time to embrace love.
Love is from above.
let it adorned your heart like pearls upon your neck.

Wear it for all to see.
When you do, love will outlive hate.
Like the sand by the seashore, learn to let love
reside inside your heart.

Love, love, wonderful love, the kind that comes only from above.

Bow your heads and say a prayer
that we will find a way to light the torch of loving one another.

Love is stronger than hate.
Grab a plate of forgiveness.
Let's get together and start loving each other
in the name of forgiving each other.

Love is all about, loving everyone,
including yourself.

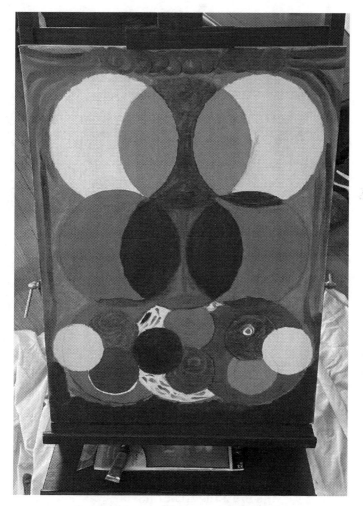

Abstract art by Yvonne White.

65

To Impeach or Not

Sick and tired of all the talk about impeachment.
All this empty talk about impeachment
is like a mother who keeps promising her children
that she is going to bake white macadamia cookies for them.

But instead of baking the cookies,
like she kept promising,
she only bakes parchment paper.

To impeach or not to impeach.
Tired of listening to the voiceless preacher telling his weary members
to hear what he have to say about the lies he is telling,
using the bully pulpit to spread division.

Tired of listening to the political pit bulls
trying to pull the wool over our eyes
and breaking sticks into our ears
to keep us in the basement of stupidity

while they massage us with juices of lies and deceptions,
trying to impregnate us with ejaculation from
their seed of white nationalist.

You are not Jim Jones.
You'd better watch your tone.
Law and order have a bone to pick with you.

Tired of listening to the big, bad wolf hiding under
Grandma's blanket, wearing a Putman jacket,
trying to deceive us
even as you treat the rest of the world like they
are just a whirlwind that no one can see.

You are on a quest to cut us off from the rest of the world,
from those who still have a conscience.

Using us as convenient to give you wings to fly to the heights
that no human has ever reached,
to sit in the seat of an earthly god next to the heavenly God.

Tired of watching you selling us out.
You are like a pimp: all you can see is your big, fat bank account.

You don't give a damn about hungry, hurting
children and weeping mothers.

You are a modern-day monster acting like a gangster,
sliding down the banister of hate and division,
with your machine gun spraying everyone with bullets
of hate and destruction.

Tired of you using us like sausage between your bun,
just so you can have fun at the expense of innocent children
dying at the border of hate and confusion.

You are living in a world of delusion.
Like Lucifer, you have come to your own conclusion.

Leave it up to you, you will destroy the world and its inhabitants
just so you can carry out your rant and
chant to bring back law and order,
giving you the power to claw away the rights of human justice for all.

All so you can have a ball,
becoming the wrecking ball.
Have you ever heard about the day of reckoning
that the good Lord talks about?

Like a cobra, you keep hissing and pissing out venom,
holding your minions by their balls,
telling them that they have to run to your beckoning,
calling to build a wall of hate and mistrust.

You don't care who get swallowed up
by the avalanche of your imagination
about immigrant spreading germs,
taking turns churning and turning on the light of darkness.
So in the name of saving America,
you are trying to destroy the fiber of democracy
in the quest of achieving autocracy.

Trying to control all branches of the government
while you take great pleasure in listening to the lamentation
of children ripped from the arms of their mothers.

Sad to say, but if Bob Marley was here,
you would hear him say many more will have to suffer,
many more will have to die.
Don't ask him why.

Tired of all the talk of impeachment
while many are still sitting in the basement of poverty and stupidity,
trying to hold on to gravity,
listening to celebrities talk about cyberbullies,
telling us to be the best
even as they turn back the hands of time.

Working without paying them fair wages,
waging war in the name of peace,
handing out pieces of peace in the name of peace and unity.

Why are you trying to burst our eardrums from
the tintinnabulation of your rhetoric?
Licking turmeric off the floor,
expecting more time,
some say to commit more crimes.

Dissecting the minds of the people programming them
into believing that you have to rule with might,
that you are always right.

You are the only one who knows how to make grater cake.
Many are standing in the food line looking for a hand up
while Hollywood and Bollywood have a huge stake
in the neighborhood, selling us their ideas,

leaving us to wade in the water of underdevelopment,
cursing people who get food stamps,
vowing to get rid of entitlement for their own enrichment.

Mr. Bollywood and Mrs. Hollywood,
you are not the ones treating people like rejects.
I hereby dare you to start a project
to help the helpless pay for their insurance.

Why can't you help feed some hungry children
and pay for college for some poor children
who have no one to help them?

Why can't we get together and break down the wall
between the haves and the have-nots?

Tired of waiting on impeachment.
Let's talk about making peach cobbler
and sharing it with the world.
Then we would not have to worry about anyone running
away from their country in order to survive.

To impeach or not to impeach depends on who is giving the speech.
I hope within my heart that peace is within reach.

66

In a World

we are living in a world
filled with sadness and trying to undress you
and take away your sanity.
How do you sanitize your mind?
How do you climb out of the strongholds of depression?
You ask yourself,
What is the difference
between depression and oppression?

Oppression is external.
Depression, to me, is internal,
the unwinnable internal war you try to fight by yourself.

The kind that makes you want to eat too much, or not enough.

Depression can hold you down.
It can turn you into a food addict, a drug addict,
even an alcoholic or a church addict.

It will hold you down and hand you the verdict of guilt,
of not being good enough or strong enough to fight depression
while you ask yourself what you can do to hold on to your sanity.

When will you find the strength to fight for freedom,
freedom from depression,
freedom from addiction?

This, my friend, is not a rendition.
Addiction comes in many different forms.
In a world filled with sadness and chaos,
how can you avoid becoming addicted to one thing or another?

67

Well of Evil

Are you still drinking from the well of hate?
Are you still thirsty for more blood?

Bob Marley said it well:
Many more will have to suffer,
many more will have to die.
Is anyone even asking why?

A dark cloud of hate is drifting across the nation,
a thick, dark cloud called hate and decision.

Where are the visionaries?
Have you seen the missionaries of peace and love,
the kind of love that comes only from above?

Stop drinking from the well of evil.
The veil is ripped apart; a spirit of hate and fear
has climb aboard in the hearts of people
who want to change the color of the nation,
retaliating against the maker of the human race.

It is a disgrace to think that self-made god is
trying to change the face of God.

Are you still too blind to see what is going on? It will not
be too long before the nation will step back in time
to the days where whites ruled,
when black folks were subhuman,
where the person with the biggest gun shall prevail.
The sad part is there will be no place to run
because white supremacists have friends in high positions.
They are positioning themselves for anarchy,
trying really hard to get rid of democracy.

This is the legacy of the "united whites" of you-know-who.
Are you still drinking from the well of hate?

68

Kindness

What is kindness?
Who teaches kindness?
Is kindness only about being kind to the people you like,
or is it about treating everyone with kindness?

If you ask me, kindness is a language that
everyone should learn to speak.
Whose responsibility it is to enroll them?

The younger generation is in the school of kindness.
it starts for a child in the mother's womb—
the thing she does or doesn't do,
the words she says or doesn't say.

We all have to strive to be kind.
Even when our animal instinct is pushing us
into being unkind, try to be kind.
First of all, be kind to yourself.

69

The Writing Is on the Wall

The writing is on the wall. the writing is on the wall.
Who are you going to call? Who are you going to call?
Stop killing the children! Stop killing the children!
No children, no future, no children, no future.
Close the blood mills, close the blood mills.
Stop grinding the bones of our people, stop
grinding the bones of our people.

The writing is on the wall, the writing is on the wall.
Where are the leaders of the free world?
Where is the leader of the country?

Are they sitting on the wall, sending out the call to one and all
who are looking for a reason to get rid of
people they don't like, whom they deem as invaders?
Telling them that it is okay to crush the bones
of people they deem troublemaker.

The writing is on the wall, the writing is on the wall.
We are looking for crusaders to stand up
to the invaders of peace and love.

It is a time for us to rise above the
whimpering whispers of hate.

Close the blood mills!
Close the blood mills!
Till the soil of love and understanding.
Let's make it our undertaking.
We need a new awakening of equality for all,
Brace yourself; it is going to get worse.

It is going to get worse, the writings on the wall.
The writing is on the wall.
Who are you going to call?
The writing is on the wall.

70

Remember When

Remember when remembering was fun?
When the sun would be on your chest, and your soul was at rest?
Now you are being put to the test.
The journey you're on is long.
You long for better days as you gaze back in.

Looking for happier times, when life was simple.
You were always laughing, showing your dimples
with perfect teeth that was as white as cotton
before they were stained with coffee.

Remember when you had no wrinkles on your freckles?
It didn't bother you when you were carefree, free from worrying.
Now, you worry about how to stop worrying
even as people tell you that you must leave your troubles at Jesus's feet.

Remember when you could go to church
and leave the troubles of the world at the front door
while you worship the Father of life?

Not anymore. Too many Christians are busy
worshiping at the shrine of their earthly god,
ganging up on those who refuse to worship their god.

Remember when those three Hebrew boys were thrown into the fire
because they refused to worship the earthly god?

At that time, the God they served showed up in the fire with them,
and not even a hair on their head was burned.
So the earthly kind made a decree that everyone
must worship the God of those three boys.

Remember when life was simple,
and simpletons were not elected to the highest office of the land?
When people genuinely loved from their hearts,
and our hearts were burning with love for one another?

When we could disagree but still agree
that everyone has their own point of view?

Remember when we didn't want to pluck out anyone's eyes
just because we don't see eye to eye?

Remember when remembering was fun,
and some of us would eat funnel cake and lick our fingers
without worrying about COVID-19?

Remember when kids would glide down the slides,
and there was a parade, and they would march in a band
and throw candies at the side of the road?

Oh! how everything has changed. Seems like a lifetime ago
that we were able to roam the store,
shopping and talking to random strangers,
complaining about some simple things like the weather.

Remember when you didn't have to stand six feet apart,
and you could wear your favorite lipstick?

Now, you are asked to wear a mask to slow the spread of COVID-19.
Some believe that they have the right to not wear a mask.
They would rather go to the bars and drink from a glass.
I get it. Yes, it is what it is.

Some people have rights, and they are allowed to do as they please,
so they go around maskless and clueless,
spreading COVID-19 while they sneeze,
because they were made to believe that COVID-19 is a hoax.

Meanwhile, some people have no rights.
To think that so many people didn't have to die
if all of us would listen to the science.

Remember when remembering was fun?
When you would go to the fair,
the kids would ride on different rides,
screaming at the top of their lungs.

When you would eat funnel cake and lick your fingers,
and you could go to Suzie and buy a tenderloin sandwich
served up with a magic trick by Troy.

Smacking your lips, enjoying cheese curds,
curling your fingers around a glass of Pepsi,
sipping and listening to what has been said.
Remember when remembering was fun?

71

What's Going On?

What's going on? Has the world going mad?
You know that things are bad when nature starts
to scream out louder than a fire alarm
as she sounds the alarm, telling us to stop and take stock.

Alaska is hot. What's up with that?
The earth is shaking, Mother Earth is breaking,
she is baking her pie. Enough is enough!
Even as the tanks of hostility sit on the street of the mall
at the president's beck and call,
waiting to have another day in the sun with an army
and watching a marching band.

Jim Crow giving orders,
children are in captivity at the borders of
hostility of hate and injustice.
Politicians are still speaking from both corners of their mouths
like mumbling fools, trying to act cool.

The marching band of insensitivity is on the move,
evoking fear upon defenseless children,
who are way too young to understand what they did wrong

to be treated like wanted criminals by a country and a people
who call themselves the home of the brave and the free.

Showing more love and compassion for your animals
while treating those innocent children like they are cannibals
coming to eat up your flesh and spit out your bones.

Stand up and speak truth to power.
Michael Vick went to prison for dog fighting.
Vick lost his job because animal lovers put on their
boxing gloves and fought for justice for the dogs.

If animals have rights,
can you really be so heartless toward those innocent children
who are placed in cages at the border of injustice?

Where is your compassion toward God's children?
He made animals and people.
Have you ever read anywhere in the Bible
that he sent his Son to die on the cross for animals?
It was for human beings that he died.
Where is your compassion for God's children?
Hey! Hey! What's going on in America?

America, have you lost your compassion? You will pay a price.
There's a God, and he listens, he never falls asleep.
He said it would be better for a millstone to be hung
around your neck for you to drown yourself in the sea
than to hurt one of his children.
America! America! God is watching.

72

Garbage

Garbage in the mind clogs your brain, allowing to lag behind.
You need to find the courage to deal with all
that is going on inside your head.

When you put your head on your pillow at night,
does the light inside your head start to shine really bright,
stopping you from falling asleep?

Garbage. If the mind will keep you up at nights,
your blood pressure will rise, so be wise
and find a way to clear the clutter inside your mind.
Garbage in, garbage out. You'd better look out,
get the garbage out before it starts to stink inside your mind.

73

What Are You Going to Do?

What are you going to do now that you know what to do?
Will you continue to play the blame game in
the quest to be a leader of stupidity,
stripping away the dignity of your soul one lie after the other?

What are you going to do now that you know that he's lying to you?
Will you still continue to act like you don't have
a clue while silencing your conscience?

If you don't know what a conscience is,
then I guess that you have already killed it.

What are you going to do?
Will you continue to act like a five-year-old
toddler trying to get what you want
and not caring about the feelings of anyone else?

Telling yourself that you're self-made—
what does it even mean to be self-made?
Sounds like madness to me.
How can a person even try to fool themselves that they are self-made?

The only thing that you make is a mockery of your indigestion,
suggesting that no one helps you get to where you are,
expecting others to run to your beck and call,
creating mayhem while the church says, "Amen."

What are you going to do now that you know
people are not always really who they say they are?
You have to look beyond the color of the blonde hair.

Don't mean nothing. Black could be white, and white could be black,
so step back, listen, and learn.
Don't you dare turn away from me.
Look me in the eyes,
because the eyes are the window to the soul.

What are you going to do now that you know what to do?

74

When the Heavens Speak

When the heavens speak,
the earth trembles with fear of the unknown.
The sea world is tucked away beneath the reach of the naked eyes,
yet the mighty ocean experiences the turmoil of the spinning world.

The animal kingdom knows how to care
for their own kind and survive.
The ones who call themselves human keep acting
like they are just common flies without brains,
draining the land of its natural beauty in the quest
to create beauty that is human-made.

Filling the ocean with plastic bottles,
destroying the ozone layers with all our cell phone batteries.
Lord, please help us to be kind to the earth.
Remind us that the world can survive without us,
but we are not able to live without the resources of the earth.

75

Nothing New

Where there is nothing new under the sun,
people live and people die.
We fight, we make up.
It is all part of the way we are made up.

Some people are happy, some are sad, some
blame the sadness on Satan.
Some people love being sad;
they like to bring the sadness to your front door.

There is nothing new under the sun.
Babies are born, they grow up, and then they die,
depending on who you are and where you are from.

You are gone. Some people will miss you.
But if no one misses you, I am sure you will not care,
because you will have no way of knowing if anyone misses you.
There is nothing new under the sun.

76

What Is Life?

What is life if you don't take your slice
by learning to feast at the table of peace?
If we don't learn how to get to know who we are,
we will become robots trying to pull happiness out of the sky,
walking on eggshells and getting mad when we break them.

What can we do to get rid of mayhem?
Sometimes there's nothing you can do to stop the flow of confusion.
Your best bet is not to allow it to infuse you,
robbing you of happiness while wasting your lives
looking for external peace and contentment.

What is life if every day, we live in strife,
creating illusion and confusion,
becoming disillusioned, listening to disinformation,
deregulating our brains, pouring our senses
into the jar of nonsensical nonsense,
draining our internal swamps at the front door of our neighbors?

Swapping out reasonings in this reason of
anything and everything goes,

forgetting about the fact that we are so posed
to be looking out for each other.

Why do we make it our business to know everyone's business,
trying to fix everyone else while wasting away in
hopes of one day reaching our destination?

Wasting away from the inside, standing on the sideline
of indecision at the concession table in the attic of the mind
while meddling with the memories of yesterday
and letting the moment pass us by, even as we ask why.

Why ask questions we already know the answers to?
What is life if we forget that it is not really ours?
It can be taken away before you get a chance to say,
Sorry for letting it pass you by.

Take the time to live while you are living.
Please don't forget to forgive.

77

Greatest Fear

When your greatest fear is that you hope
they don't bring the protest to your community,
then you, my friend, don't really have very much to be afraid of.

When your greatest fear is that you are in a park,
and a black man told you that you should put your dog on a leash,
and you unleash your fury on him, telling him
that you are going to call 911 and tell them
that a black man is attacking you and you are afraid for your life,
then you, my friend, have nothing to worry about.

A few weeks after a policeman kneeled on the neck of a black man,
taking his life without even think twice for the whole world to see.

Hope you know, my friend, that this country is heading for trouble,
and if that don't bother you,
then I guess I really don't have a clue as to what grief is.

When you have no empathy, and you cannot find
it in your heart to try to understand

how a mother of any race feels whose son has been shot
by people who are hired to serve and protect them,
I guess you have nothing to worry about.

If you get offended that a black mother whose son has
been shot dead is speaking up about injustice,
then you, my friend, really don't have anything to worry about.

When all you see is what the naked eye can see,
then you, my friend, are living in a sea of sedation
without facing reality that the spirit of hate is residing in our hearts.
Just so you know, that hatefulness will rob us of internal peace.

When you are more concerned about a dog who is left inside a hot car
than about a black man whose life was taken from him,
and for what? Just because he's black and talking back.

If you don't know, let me tell you: anarchy will take over.
The fire and fury of lies and hate will start to blaze.
The smoke of hatred will burn your eyes.

Many more people are going to do die
while politicians continue to lie just so they can
get by, trying to divide the nation.

When all is said and done, you and I and everyone
will one day have to answer to the one who created the human soul.
Then you and I cannot give him any bullshit
that there are good people on both sides.

The day will come when you will stop liking them,
and then they will come for you. Mark my words.

The day will come when your conscience tells
you what you're seeing is wrong,
and when you open your mouth to say it like you see it,
they will come for you.

They don't really like you.
They just pretend to like you,
because they think you stand for what they stand for.

Mark my words: when the day comes,
and you change your mind and vote for someone else,
Watch out.
You will see then, and you will know what
it feels like to feel like an outsider.

Until that day comes,
I guess you will not know what I am saying.

When your greatest fear is you hope that they
don't bring the protest to your front door,
I guess that you really don't have anything to worry about.

78

All I Can Hear

When all I can hear is the voice of my child
calling out my name, rumbling inside my head,
but my heart stopped feeling, at least for now,
no, I have not gone cold.
In fact, I think that I am actually getting bolder,
not because I'm strong but because I am so weak.

I have asked God, Please carry me through this
nightmare that I am going through.
Many are of the opinion that I have gone cold.

I really just want to fall off the grid. Feels like someone is
grinding up my bones in the mill of bitter memories
while I trying to shield my mind from the cold reality
that I will never again see my daughter in this life.

Losing my daughter is the most painful thing
that has ever happened to me,
but this will not go away—or will it?

I feel like I just need to find a way
to hide myself from the pain.

How do I?
How do I cope when it feels like someone
has a thick rope around my neck,
choking the life out of me?
Silently I scream,

wondering when the pain will subside.
You don't have to tell me life will never be the same,
because all I am hearing
is the voice of my child calling my name,
rumbling inside my head,
preventing me from sleeping in my bed.

79

Who Are You to Judge Me?

Who are you to judge me and tell me who to be and not to be?
Why are you so busy interfering in my affairs?
My life is not a fairytale. I have much to fear,
but I choose to walk away from my fears.

I am not looking back, so whatever you have to say to me,
have the balls to look me into the eyes
and tell me what you have to say to my face.
You are not the only one trying to finish the race.

Who are you to keep belittling me,
making me out to be a monster without feelings,
when you have no way of knowing what makes tick?
You are like ticks on my back slowly draining my blood,
Telling me that I am not welcome in your neighborhood.

Are you not tired of swimming in by blood?
Who are you to judge me?

80

A White

Why are you always a white man wearing a long white gown,
but your eyes are always looking so sad?
Your lips are perfect and thin,
leaving me to start thinking that I am a bastard child.
How comes I don't look anything like you?
Your nose is straight;
mine is big and wide, takes up most of my face.

Why are you always a white man?
I never see anyone paint a black Jesus.
If I was an artist, I would paint you with a thick, wide nose.
The nail marks in your hands would be bigger
because I know that you are strong,
so I know that they didn't use any tiny nails to nail you to the cross.

Why are you always a white man telling me
to take up the cross and follow you?
The preacher says if I confess my sins, you
will make me whiter than snow.

What I want to know is, How do you sell a white Jesus to
a black nation who has been oppressed by whites?

Slave masters calling sin black and making us feel
like we were created to take out the garbage
and that our lives don't matter as a matter of fact.

They are trying to control us,
trying to put a spell on us,
trying to shrink our brains
to keep us under their feet,

saying we don't measure up to the heights of being human;
by that, they mean because we are not white.

I know Jesus. Yes, I really do.
You created me in your image.
Your love for your children is color-blind.

I don't need a blind to hide from the face
of Jesus in order to hide my sin.

All I have to do is confess my sin to you and let you do the rest.
I know that the preacher always says Jesus would
cleanse me and make me whiter than snow.

But Jesus, I don't want to be white.
I still cannot figure out why they always painted
you as a white man with a sad face.

Jesus, I know that you already know I don't
really want to be made white.
I don't want to be right.

I want only to be able to celebrate my blackness
with wide nose and big lips.
Will you please make them stop spilling our blood
like they are sipping on Kool-Aid or watermelon wine?

Why are you always a white man with sad eyes?

We praise him just because he is God.
The blessings come down when our praises go up,
When we bow down before the one who creates the heavens,
the one who blows the wind, and the leaves fall off the trees.

He is the one who dries our tears!
That is why I praise him!
Do you have a reason to praise him?

81

When

By: *Yvonne White*

When you feel like running away from the whole world,
and your mind is like a globe filled with unwanted feelings,
splashing around inside your head,
keeping you awake in bed with your heart feeling like lead.

When you go to work and work really hard,
smiling, trying to be happy and make others laugh,
yet your heart is like a dry bark,
and the blood inside your veins is getting thicker
while your mind is overloaded with sadness and distress.

You dress to impress,
yet you can't seem to find a seamstress
to make you a gown to hide.

You frown while unhappy thoughts flows through your mind,
making you want to get lost in a place where no one knows you.

You are crying on the inside and smiling on the outside,

standing behind a thick cloud with a crowded mind,
meddling with fear, wondering if anyone even cares.

You long to have a mother's tender touch,
to be able to tell her anything and everything that is bothering you,
but you refuse to bother her because you never really get to know her.

When and how shall you start to open up,
when you feel like you just want to run away from the whole world?

82

You Hop on a Bus

You hop on a bus heading to nowhere,
telling yourself that when you get there,
no one will care about you or where you came from.
But what will you tell the person inside of
you who is tired of running away?

They're only trying to get to know who they were meant to be.

How does it feel to be living on the street called nowhere,
sleeping on a bench at a bus park
with your shoes under the bench,
holding your hands shut tight across your chest?
Are you holding on to something that you don't want to lose?

How did you become homeless?
Was it because of meth, cocaine, or was it heroin?
Did they all promise to take you away from your troubles,
telling you that you can learn to be your own hero
with just another sniff?
Was that one of your sales pitch? No!

You find yourself in a ditch, being a wimp with a stick,
wishing that you had listened to that one
person who loves you so much.
Even though your mother is dead, her prayers are still alive.
Why don't you hop on the bus that is called reality?

83

Beginning

Iam beginning to understand that life is not worth living.
If you don't know what you are living for,
how easy it is to forget why you were born.

We adorn ourselves in robes of self-pity,
slipping on our own slimy thoughts,
drinking a broth of bitterness.

Are you living in a fool's paradise,
trying to buy happiness off the back of sadness?
That little red dress is not for you.
Build your own medium red dress.

I am beginning to understand that you enter into life screaming,
and you go out kicking.
But before you go, lend a helping hand to some helpless child,
give a smile to someone,
pat someone on the shoulder,
let them know that you care.

Hug someone. You may never know
when you will be the one needing a kind word or a hug.
I am beginning to understand what life is all about.

84

Window of Expectation

Sitting at the window of expectation,
waiting with anticipation for my guardian angel
to come rescue me.

Sitting in a corner by the window of expectation,
waiting with bated breath for her to come
and take me away from this prison.
While I waited for her, my heart ached for the love of a mother.

Sitting in the room of confusion,
trying to come to my own conclusion.

She is never coming back
She is never, ever coming back.
I brace myself for what is to come.
I understand it well!
Yes, I understand it well.
My back is against the wall,
my back is against the wall.
I am afraid and lonely.

I have no one to call.
What shall I do?
Heaven knows that I don't have a clue.

Sitting at the window of anticipation,
suffering from constipation.

Holding on to sad emotions
while erecting a tent of unbelief,
trying to hide my grief.

They keep on telling me that I'm a drama queen
who is seeking attention.

I don't need anyone to tell me who I am
or what I'm trying to get.
What the heck!

Why can't you seem to get it?
I am just a little girl
waiting for my mother to show up
and take me home where I belong.

Sitting at the window of anticipation,
waiting for my mother to come and take me home.

Something in my heart tells me she is never, ever coming back.

Sitting at the window of expectation,
waiting with bated breath.

85

Decluttering the Mind

Yesterday, the day Joe Biden and
Kamala Harris were elected to office,
I was decluttering my room.
My mind was not an anything special.
As of late, I have been blocking everything
and anything from my mind.

My mind is like a junkyard that I tossed everything in,
then when I lie in bed at night,
it's like a giant salad bowl.
I toss around everything, trying to line them
up in order of date and time.

Let's get back to yesterday while I was decluttering my room.

I found an old birthday card from the year 2000.
I got it from a couple when I was a live-in
nanny, looking after their little girl.

After reading it, I started crying—really crying,
You see, I have been sweeping my feelings
under a rug for almost all my life.

That was my way of not falling apart.
I know that is a horrible way to deal with your feelings,
but that was my way of coping.
Not saying it is right, but that is where I am in my life right now.

It is almost like I fell asleep and walked around in my house.
My emotion drags me back to the year 2000,
when I lost myself, when the real me died,
and I became a dead woman walking, taking up space.

God is telling me that he wants to heal my emotion,
but for that to happen, I have to revisit my fast.

I am sure you are wondering what happened in 2000.
In 2000, I lost my job.
At the time, I had three children, two girls and one son,
who were depending on me for everything.

Jamaica is not like the United States of America,
where you have a lot of programs to help single mothers, like food
stamps, that can help out you if you find yourself in a jam.

The father of my children, my ex-husband, had
already ridden off into the sunset,
started a new family even before I filed for divorce.

There I was struggling to find food, no money to pay rent and utilities,
and no money in my bank account.
I ended up sending my children to three different places.

My children were my life; they made me forget
about the way I was treated by my mother.
I didn't know anything about her.
I knew that she didn't hate me,
but still I was never able to tell if she loves me.

Will my children hate me for abandoning them?

I needed them as much as they needed me.
Looking back, I have come to the conclusion that
I needed them more than they needed me.

There I was, standing at the edge of insanity,
trying to cope with the reality of not being
able to take care of my children.

Not even going to try to fully explain my traumatic experience,
because it will take three books to do that.

The long and short of this tale is this:
it is because of the year 2000 that you are reading this.
I was content to be an unknown for the rest of my life
if it meant that I was able to rewrite the wrong that was done to me,
to protect my children and provide for them.
But I guess that God had other plans for my life.

He has made it clear to me that it is not
about me anymore—never was.
I am just a tool in his workshop that he is using
to reach someone, somewhere, who is going through hell.

Here I am, in 2020, twenty years after falling off the ladder of sanity,

living on the edge of insanity.
Yet no one had truly understood that I was a dead woman walking.

Now, I am writing from my painful memories to reach you,
even though I never met you.
God is telling me to tell you that you are not alone.

I am confused more than I ever.
I find myself questioning God.
Why could I have not been born into a stable family,
with a mother and father who loved each other?
In return, I would have felt love and acceptance.

Just so you know, I don't have any grievance against my parents.
It is with God.
My earthly parents had no control over what had happen to me,
so by no means am I trying to be mean to them.
I just have questions to ask.
even though I may never get any answers.

Not trying to play a blame game.
As a Christian, I am aware that my life is not a gamble.
I am loved by God,
but knowing that he loves me does not take away my pain.
Nor does it stop me from experiencing sadness or distress.

He uses them to get my attention,
But I kept hiding, not wanting to experience the painful emotions,
so I kept digging a hole to hide my feelings in.

I am a stranger to everyone in Iowa;
no one knows where I am coming from emotionally.
Yes! they know that I am Jamaican.

Yet here I am, turning into a writer.
God is not racist; he loves all his children.
If we allow him, he will turn our crises into life lessons.

At times I often feel like a tiny piece of chocolate chip
in a gallon of white milk,
yet I am able to maintain my identity.
God, in his wisdom, placed me in the middle of people
who genuinely care about me in the middle of the Midwest.

There was a time in my life when I felt like I
was a nobody, and maybe I was.
I was programed to believe that I was not good enough to have parents
who loved me, and wanted me.
What does a child know?

The world is full of people who are hurting,
which manifests itself in many forms.
People are hurting for many different reasons,
but like myself, everyone wants to change the world.
Sounds mighty good, but it will never work.

The only way we can change the world is to change our internal world.

I am not saying changing the world is a bad thing,
but if we set out on a quest to change the world

just so we can avoid dealing with our own shit,
then we are heading for deep shit.

God is using me to reach the unreachables.
Anyway, I need to get back to dealing with my own shit
that God told me is my message.

In 2000, I was homeless and had to get a job as a live-in helper,
looking after a family of four.
God provide that for me.

Funny how we limp around in life,
forgetting what it feels like to walk without limping.

Something happens to us, and we start limping.
One of our emotional feet is broken.
Then something happens again, like the death of a child.

Our good foot gets smashed, and we land on our ass.
Some of us are too proud to ask for help,
so we drag ourselves around until we start to bleed.
I am not good at opening up about how I am feeling.
I am an inside bleeder.

Sometimes I think that God is crazy.
The thing he knows you hate the most
is the thing he uses to reach you, in order to reach others.

I have so much sadness and grief accounts.
I know that I need to settle,

because the grief collector is always knocking
on the door of my emotion,
telling me that I need to settle up.
Emotionally, I am crying, Mayday! Mayday!
But no one can hear me.

So I find myself lost in the cornfield of Iowa,
lost in the corridors of my mind,
singing like the Commodores,
hiding behind a smile, walking on dynamite,
fighting with all my might to get it right,
wearing a mask to hide from COVID-19 and also to hide my pain.
Just for the sake of decluttering my mind.

86

My Daughter

My friend, my soul, my child,
you came into this world screaming
with eyes that pierced my soul.

I look into your eyes, I saw myself.
My sweet child, I did for you what my mother could not do for me.
My daughter, my soul, my friend,
If I could have traded places with you, I would have,
but it was not meant to be.

For you, I will be strong.
I will sing when I feel like I only want to cry.
For you, my child, I will find a way to change the world,
to make it a better place by changing myself first.
I will take my place in a world
where evil waits around the corner,
trying to suck the joy and happiness from our souls.

I will be strong.
I will keep singing the freedom song.
Born to shine, to strive to do what's right,
To pull someone up,

to impart wisdom that comes only from
the womb of pain and suffering.

My daughter, my child,
you are gone; I am here.
I will try to be brave, I will bear the pain
and stay clear of the blame game.
You came into my life like the morning dew.
You were not able to stick around
until you could spread your golden crystal across the sky.
I kept asking why.

My daughter, my child, my soul,
for your memory, I will create a bank account.
Daily I will deposit words of understanding.
The world will hear my voice, and they will listen
because I will command their respect.
Not because they want to give it to me,
but because I have earned it.

My daughter, my child,
I am not able to give you back your life,
however I will add value to mine
by taking time to unlock my true potential.
I will stare into the faces of those who want to see me fail.
I will show them that I am strong, brave, and proud.

My daughter, my child,
I will draw from the well of understanding
even though I don't understand why you had to go.

I will ask God to give me the strength to let you go
so I can remain in the land of the living.

My daughter, my friend, my soul,
goodbye for now, until we meet on the other side.

About the Author

Yvonne is a Jamaican living in Iowa. She writes and sings to stay sane, which helps her rise above the deep wounds of her past. Her brain is like a reservoir filled with thoughts, some angry and some sad. The wounded little girl living inside of her is not able to remember how old she was when her virginity was taken away from her.

Yvonne has already found it in her heart to forgive others. She is now trying to find self-forgiveness. She writes from feelings deep within her belly, to hide the pain and the tears.

She hopes to help someone who is feeling like a nobody and has no one who truly understands what they are going through. She wants them to know that they are not alone. If she was able to find her voice through the tip of a pen or with her vocal chords, you can, and you will!

Yvonne is slowly finding a way to deal with her past and cope with the harsh realities that life dumps on her front porch. She is no longer licking her many wounds; rather, she is raising above the hurts and the pain that she has endured over the years, like being molested by family member and not being able to remember how old she was when her virginity was stolen.

She is overcoming the sting of rejection by her mother, even if it was only in her head. She has experienced two failed marriages and the death of two children, both of whom were thirty-three years old when they died. Her oldest daughter died in 2018, and her oldest son died in 2021, tilting her world upside down And sending her to inpatient behavioral health for a week.

She did not want to eat or speak to anyone. She didn't care whether she lived or die. While she was there, she met a young man who was twenty-eight years old, and it was almost like her son was talking through him.

Yvonne hit rock bottom, but she came full circle with the grace and goodness of God. While she was in the hospital, she heard a small voice told her that she was going to pick up painting to carry on her son's legacy.

She told herself that she was going crazy, but God is a healer! He gives you peace in the he midst of your storm. She started to do abstract painting, and that was the best therapy. It cleansed her mind.

She is trying to raise her two youngest children on her own, teaching them good morals, and keeping her home a safe haven from the use of drugs.

She has to work overtime all the time to show her children that if you put your shoulders to the wheel, even though you get a raw deal, you don't have to spin the welfare wheel of fortune.

With the help of God, she has learned to smile gracefully and has turned the other cheek to some people who think that because she is an immigrant, she has no rights, even though she is not breaking any laws.

Yvonne is embracing the pain and sadness. With the help of God, she knows that she will overcome whatever comes her way, even if it takes a while.

Printed in the United States
by Baker & Taylor Publisher Services